The *Positively You!* Discovery Journal

JINGER
HEATH

St. Martin's Griffin ⚏ New York

Book design by Donna Sinisgalli

ISBN 0-312-25465-2

First Edition: January 2000

10   9   8   7   6   5   4   3   2   1

The
*Positively
You!*
Discovery
Journal

ALSO BY
JINGER HEATH

Positively You!

To my daughter,

Brittany Elizabeth Heath.

May your own journey

be a celebration of growth.

Contents

Contents

Contents

Special thank-yous to my special family

St. Martin's Press

⚘

My Editor, Elizabeth Beier

⚘

My Literary Agent, Jan Miller

⚘

Lynn Adler, for her invaluable help on the manuscript

⚘

And the thousands of amazing women
around the world I've had the privilege to
know and who have positively inspired my
own journey.

Introduction:
The Journey to Becoming *Positively You*

Greetings, sister traveler! Speaking to you from this page I feel as though I am meeting you at a crossroads. As you hold this journal in your hands, it's your *heart* that holds the answers you seek for your life's direction. If you don't believe that now, my heart's desire is that your journey through these pages will help you re-discover your own answers—your own *dreams*—so you can believe in yourself once more.

I've learned some simple but life-changing lessons in the course of my own journey. I shared those simple truths with other women in my first book, *Positively You!* The response was so overwhelming; it became clear that a companion journal would make a real difference in helping even more women believe in themselves again.

An old Chinese proverb teaches us: *"What I hear, I forget. What I see, I remember. What I do, I know."*

This DISCOVERY JOURNAL is about *doing*.

To be more specific, this journal is about *you* doing the doing. No doubt you've heard plenty of life-changing theories, techniques, and philosophies. And certainly you've seen endless examples—in person as well as in print, on film, or on live TV—of how others have changed their lives. But only when you've actually *done* the "change your thinking" work—only then, can you truly *know* the "change your life" experience.

That's why it's important for me to describe this DISCOVERY JOURNAL as a "course of action" rather than simply a "workbook." No way am I going to let you fall into the easy trap of thinking once you've written your thoughts in the book, you've taken the action you need to take! (Or if you're like me, you may have a knack for tricking yourself into thinking you've made progress simply through the act of purchasing such a book.)

Believe me—have DISCOVERY JOURNAL, will travel. Take heart in knowing that the personal discoveries you're about to make in these pages definitely will inspire your course of action with the get-up-and-go that you thought had long since got-up-and-went. You'll count it one of the best time and money investments you've made in your life. How do I know? True to the proverb I quoted earlier—"What I do, I know."

I've taken the very course of action you're about to take and that has made all the difference. I have turned my life around; from taking a very roundabout way to a destination that was uncertain at best, to being a woman on a mission. A dual mission, actually—to live my own dreams and to help other women do the same. Are you game?

It's those things that I've come to know by doing—those tools that I've learned to put to good use—that form the foundation of this DISCOVERY JOURNAL. As I've learned to use the tools, I've learned to change the way I think. And that is how I've made real changes in my life.

There's no reason you can't do the same.

I count it an honor and a privilege to stand at this place and point the way by bringing you a proven course of action. May it cheer you onward and upward.

There are unlimited horizons for each of us.

And we are capable of finding our way there.

J.L.H.
1999

Preparing

for the

Journey

How to Pack
and Unpack for the
Positively You Life

Remember what it was like when you were a little girl preparing to go on a school field trip, heading to summer camp or off to a stay with a favorite aunt or grandparent? There was always a list of things to do and items to bring along. Do you recall how, as you got your things together and ready to go, you were filled with a sense of expectancy and delight at the very thought of all the new discoveries you were about to make?

There was great comfort found in the act of getting ready—of preparing for the journey. Actions you took before leaving helped ensure you would have a favorable trip and a great time once you arrived.

Granted, the journey of life is hardly comparable to that of a day trip to the zoo or a week spent camping in the woods. Still, experience teaches us it's smart to prepare. To know what to pack—and what to leave behind.

Of course, I know you are not just starting out; that you are well into your life's journey. And I understand how the experiences of your childhood, combined with life choices you've made as an adult, greatly influence the list of "things"—positives and negatives—you've carried with you on the journey thus far.

That's why it's a good idea to take a personal inventory. As you record thoughts and feelings on the pages to come, *your* words will provide the compass you need to find your way back to celebrating yourself and believing in *you* again.

Fueled by that powerful belief, you will have all the drive you need to stay on track and really live the life that is *positively you,* instead of postponing it. That's why I want you to reach inside yourself right this very minute and muster up some of that child-like "I just can't *wait* for tomorrow" kind of energy you had an endless supply of in earlier years.

Let's get on with the business of getting ready for the adventure that awaits you! May you find comfort—and the delight of anticipation—in these "preparing for the journey" pages.

What to Leave Behind

I encourage you to mentally "unpack" some bags to make room for the things you definitely don't want to make the journey without. On second thought, I don't just encourage you to do this; I insist.

I know, I know.

You don't just say "POOF!" and make all the negatives in your life disappear. But you can make up your mind to be more conscious of when the negatives try to sneak in and do their dirty work. Trust me, this is not brain surgery. It just sounds difficult because most of us are pretty rusty in the old "change your think-ing" department.

Think of it this way: How much closer to living your dreams

could you be if you spent as much time making up your mind (or in other words, "changing your thinking") as you do, say . . . making up your face or choosing what to wear? What about the time you invest in deciding everything from which movie to rent to which car to buy? The time you spent selecting your last vacation destination? Or the deliberating you do over how to save for your child's college education? There are so many thoughts that affect so many actions in our lives.

Still, we spend so little if any time preparing our minds with the kind of thinking that has the greatest potential to change our lives from the inside out. Here's an example of what I'm talking about. Let's say I'm heading into the office for a board meeting at our company.

Before, during, and after getting ready to go somewhere, I am doing my mental packing and unpacking for the day's events. In my head it sounds something like this: "Okay, Jinger. You've got a board meeting today. Let's be sure to check any negativity and self-doubt at the door. Bring plenty of positive energy. And you know today's meeting will probably go long, so throw in some extra sense of humor while you're at it . . ."

See what I mean? In the time it takes me to mentally pack and unpack those essentials, I become more prepared and filled with anticipation for the "adventure" to come. For the brief time I invest in changing—or adjusting—my thinking, I gain so much in the way I have changed my life for that day. And since I am Chairman of the Board, that's a good thing. (The rest of our board members experience the difference too.)

Try this "change your thinking" approach the next time you get ready to meet with an individual or group. Maybe there's one person who's a particular challenge to you. A co-worker, a friend. Maybe even your own child or your mother! Does is seem like you somehow always miscommunicate with each other? You don't "connect"? Does your relationship with that person require more effort? More maintenance?

That's okay.

You'll handle the situation just fine as long as you mentally prepare to not let that person's negative "baggage" affect your own thinking.

Before you encounter this person (or group), remind yourself to take your time. To breathe. And to leave behind fear, self-doubt, and negativity (or whatever negatives are weighing you down). Then, with every breath (go ahead—try it!) fill your heart and mind with the positive energy that will help you make the encounter a good one.

Changing your thinking and changing your life happen one moment at a time. Just as a commitment to practice applies to diet and exercise—the same principle applies to your mental well-being. To be healthy and fit for the rest of your life requires healthful eating habits and hearty physical activity—for the rest of your life. Ditto when it comes to your thinking.

Here's another way to think about the mental unpacking process. Ever notice how it takes only one really soiled piece of laundry to taint an entire suitcase of clothes? Think about that next time you're getting ready to walk into a meeting or sit down to have a heart-to-heart with your spouse. It takes only one really strong, negative feeling of fear, guilt, or self-doubt to wreak major havoc with the way we think about ourselves and our potential for change. Not to mention the negative effect on our ability to communicate.

My advice for traveling the road to *positively you*? Travel light.

That's why it's so important for us to unpack our bags before we head into the adventure of each day! The negatives weigh us down—physically, spiritually, and emotionally.

The following exercise is the beginning of a makeover that works from the inside out. When you start mentally unpacking the heaviness of self-doubt you've been toting around all these years, you'll be amazed at how much easier it will be to take action. You'll have the personal resolve you need to keep changing your life. Your friends will notice a new "glow" about your appearance. You'll meet each new day with more exuberance, less exhaustion.

Following is my list of Top 10 Leave-Behinds. Read each one. Think about how it relates to your own life. And add your own "unpacking thoughts" in the journal space provided. Do this and I promise you will experience a major, *positive* energy surge.

Mentally unpack the negatives from your thoughts through the act of "leaving them behind" on the written page. Consider the following exercise the beginning of a daily practice of mental preparation. In the pages to come, you'll have the opportunity to explore these issues further.

Top 10 Leave-Behinds

1. Fear . . . **It comes in a zillion shapes and sizes.** I don't suggest it's possible or even desirable to completely leave fear behind. Some fears teach us valuable lessons; other kinds of fear actually protect us. But it's the fears that set up residence inside the way we think—the fears that keep us from becoming all that we can be—those are the ones we can be more conscious of each day.

Do you have a fear that's so much a part of your thinking you can't imagine living without it? One of the fears I've had to really work at unpacking all my life has been the plain old fear of failure. And one of the ways I've learned to unpack that fear is to focus on my successes—from my children, to our family's health, to our company's success in business. In learning to banish my own fears (a daily practice!), I continue to learn new ways to accomplish my dreams.

What about you? Go ahead. Writing it down brings you one step closer to leaving it behind. *Some fears I could stand to unpack include my fear of* (i.e., fear of failure, fear of speaking in public, fear of rejection, fear of intimacy, fear of what others think of me, etc.) . . . _____

_____

_____

_____

_____

_____

2. Procrastination ... **A "symptom" of fear.** I tend to do this subconsciously. And as with other bad habits, one has to admit she's a procrastinator, before she can unpack the pesky tendency! Procrastination is about the things we avoid. Now there's a list just waiting to be "unpacked" and written down. *The list of things I tend to avoid includes* (i.e., bookkeeping, house-cleaning, getting a mammogram, working in my DISCOVERY JOURNAL, committing to an exercise regimen, etc.) ...

_____

_____

_____

_____

_____

_____

_____

Tempted to put off this part of the exercise? Don't you do it! Remember, this is a "top ten" list, which means these ten issues are biggies we all face—you, me, the biggest celebrities, and most important minds. I've found it's whatever I'm most insecure about that I procrastinate or avoid the most. Procrastination is not just about what we don't get done; it's about what we avoid thinking about.

3. Guilt ... **Talk about weighty stuff.** I still feel guilt for not taking time to have dinner with my dad the night before he died. I so clearly remember him calling me up and saying, "Hey, doll!

Come over and have some quail with me tonight." But I couldn't. I was just too caught up in the busyness of life.

He died that night! Still, as much as I regret my choice of plans for that one evening, and as sad as dwelling on the thought can make me feel, I've learned to leave behind that guilty feeling. The lesson of the experience did not go unlearned, but to carry around the guilt serves no purpose. Besides, it does not celebrate the memory of my dad. He would never have wanted such thoughts to weigh me down.

Does the weight of guilt—real, manufactured, or otherwise— slow you down? If you're like a lot of women, you struggle with feelings of guilt simply for "taking this time for *you*" as you think, read, and write in your journal. Begin now to be more conscious of guilt's paralyzing effects on your course of action.

Starting now, I will practice leaving behind my feelings of guilt for (i.e., not having spotless kitchen countertops, missing my son's last ball game because of work, living far away from my aging parents, actually taking my vacation days instead of working through them, eating two scoops of white chocolate macadamia nut ice cream last night before I went to bed, etc.) . . . _____

_____

_____

_____

_____

_____

4. Self-doubt ... **It's like driving with your foot on the brakes.** When you're always second-guessing yourself, it's hard to get very far down the road to your dreams. For many years, I was well practiced at self-doubt. My number one issue as a child was that I felt "invisible." It seemed there was nothing I could say or do to change the difficulties my family was going through. The people around me had so many challenges going on for themselves, they were just trying to survive. Consequently, I felt like I was part of the woodwork. I desperately needed to be recognized. To be *heard*.

How ironic it is that I now make my living in such a "visible" way. I appear on stage, in print, and on videos and audiotapes promoting our company's products. I've even appeared on national television, promoting my books on programs such as *The Oprah Winfrey Show*, TNN's *Crook and Chase, The View with Barbara Walters*, and CNN's *Business Unusual.*

But as it turns out, being visible—being "celebrated"—is not the source of my self-esteem or self-assuredness. The quiet process of celebrating myself on the inside—the daily practice of trusting my instincts—enables me to "unpack" self-doubt and move on.

Try it. Begin the practice of celebrating "you." One step at a time, trust yourself and take action. Remember those times when you've said to yourself, "I just knew I should have turned right instead of left." Or, "I started to take that job offer, but I played it safe and decided to stay where I am." Oh, the ways we second-guess ourselves into a rut!

Think about the ways you doubt yourself. Write them down and start leaving them behind. *These are some of the self-doubts that consistently slow me down* (i.e., not listening to that "little voice" inside, caring too much about what other people think, etc.) . . . _____

_____

_____

_____

_____

Remember, that little voice inside you, your instinct, or your intuition—whatever you choose to call it—is a gift from God.

5. Self-criticism . . . **"I am sooo stupid!"** How many times do we say things like that to ourselves without thinking? Self-criticism is an ongoing struggle for me, but I've learned to recognize its presence in my thinking process. And that awareness helps me to be able to leave self-criticism behind.

Just think what the power of your self-critical thinking and verbalizing is doing to undermine you being all you can be. When you say, "Oh gosh! I'm so fat," or "I'm such a moron," you give yourself a double whammy. Your subconscious thinks it. Then, if you actually speak the words, you hear it again—only louder!

From now on, whenever you catch yourself thinking or saying something self-critical, make a conscious effort to rephrase your thought—even say it out loud. "I wish I'd done it differently, but I'm *not* stupid." We're all human beings. When you make a mistake, just say, "I made a mistake and I'll learn from this mistake." Write down some of the automatic self-critical sayings that pop into your head frequently so you'll be more conscious of them. *Some of the self-criticisms I want to leave behind include* (i.e., "I'm such a wimp, I can't say no," "I'm a failure," "I'm so fat." "I'm never going to accomplish my goals," etc.) . . . _____

_____

_____

_____

_____

    When's the last time you *accepted* a compliment, anyway? Celebrate yourself and start accepting who you positively are!

6. Hopelessness . . . **Leave this one behind and you won't be so tempted to abandon your course of action.** Believe me, if you're feeling hopeless about something in your life right now, that feeling will drain you of any energy or desire you have to change your life. In fact, the medical community has reported case after medical case of how negative thoughts can have a toxic effect on the body. There's no doubt that hopelessness is a negative thought.

    My feelings of hopelessness about (i.e., my career, my health, a family squabble, my ability to work through this DIS-

13

COVERY JOURNAL, etc.) *are getting me nowhere fast. Starting here, I'm leaving behind my hopelessness regarding . . .* _____

_____

_____

_____

_____

_____

7. Helplessness . . . This one's about feeling "out of control." We've all felt helpless at one time or another. Sometimes you think there's nothing you can do. You may feel overwhelmed. Of course, some aspects of life are out of our control—for instance, in the case of a serious illness of a loved one. Still, we can pray! And we can celebrate the good experiences we've had with that person.

I know from experience that the way to feel less helpless is to change the way you perceive a situation and focus on the positive. That way, you're in control. You're no longer a victim of your own feelings. I practice this all the time when I'm driving in traffic. When I'm stuck in a traffic jam in the middle of the freeway, there's not a lot I can do about it. But I can change my attitude about being stuck there. I change my thinking and I change my life for that moment. And that has a positive effect on my state of mind when I get where I'm going, too!

Remember, you are on the way to becoming *positively you.*

The feelings of helplessness will not help on your journey, so—unpack them! Then you'll be able to muster all the inner strength you need to tackle obstacles, real and imagined. *My feelings of helplessness about* (i.e., having money, succeeding as a single parent, being in control of my future, etc.) *won't help me on my journey. I'm unpacking my helpless feelings about . . .* _____

_____

_____

_____

_____

_____

8. Self-destructiveness . . . **Time for another personal testimonial.** Oh, the times I have overwhelmed, overscheduled, and overcommitted myself. Women seem to specialize in this. And, yes, such behavior absolutely *is* self-destructive. Suggestions? Alter your schedule. Try cutting it by 30 percent! At least shoot for that and you'll cut back considerably. A sure way to cut your schedule is to carefully analyze how you spend your minutes, hours, and days. Then put yourself on a time "budget." When you change the way you think about what you actually can afford to spend, it becomes easier to change your time-spending habits. You'll explore this in greater detail in the final chapter.

Of course, self-destructiveness also ranges from not getting enough rest and exercise, to *over*indulging in such areas as eating, drinking, smoking, etc. Watch out for those not-so-obvious self-destructive behaviors too, like judging, gossiping, criticizing, etc. *Ouch!*

I'm definitely unpacking my self-destructive habits like (i.e., working late every day, skipping breakfast, not making time for "play," saying "yes" when I should say "no," etc.) . . .

_____

_____

_____

_____

_____

9. Negativity . . . **Hit the "eject" button.** Pitch those old tapes you've been playing inside your head that tell you "you're too old to change your thinking, much less change your life." You know—the "scripts" you've recited to yourself all your life, like, "You're not enough," "You're alone," "Women can't do that!" Blah, blah, blah. Nix the negativity!

The negativity I most want to leave behind has to do with my (i.e., my boss, my childhood, my self-image, my daily outlook, etc.) . . . _____

_____

_____

_____

_____

10. Negative People . . . **"Get them out of your life!"** I say that to anyone I know who's having people problems. It sounds harsh, but it's the best advice I've ever followed. Let me tell you, you are heading into a downward spiral fast if you continue to let negative people into your life.

Be creative; set boundaries.

Here's an example of what to say to the negative people in your life: "I can't stay sane and continue to do things this way." Or, "That just won't work for me anymore. I've got to make some changes . . ." Stop playing caregiver to all those negative people who are bleeding you dry.

We do live in the real world, and I know we can't make all the negative people just disappear. They're everywhere—on TV news and on certain talk shows. Turn them "off." Avoid them. But we can't choose our relatives, so in that case, distance is key. (That's why some are called "distant" relatives!) If you have a relative who's really negative, it's okay to put limits on the time you spend with that person. The negative people in your life don't need to know you're limiting time with them. You can keep that to yourself and quietly draw strength from knowing you are changing your life for the better.

My journey to "positively me" will go a lot smoother if I start distancing myself from (i.e., that friend who's a real downer, that gossipy group at work, that family member who always puts me down, etc.). *I need to "unpack"* (write down their names!) . . . _____

_____

_____

_____

_____

_____

Remember that Chinese proverb: "What I hear, I forget. What I see, I remember. What I do, I know." Now that you've done this unpacking exercise, you know what a great feeling it is to leave the negatives behind on the written page. That knowledge will fuel your resolve to leave them behind again, every day.

Here's what you just unpacked:

- Fear
- Procrastination
- Guilt
- Self-doubt
- Self-criticism
- Hopelessness
- Helplessness
- Self-destructiveness
- Negativity
- Negative People

Great job!! Now let's pack the positives!

Top 10 Bring-Alongs

1. A Sense of Expectancy . . . Instead of a sense of dread.
I much prefer facing each new day with a sense of expectancy—don't you? If you've ever given birth, you have that perspective on the meaning of expectancy. You get a whole nine months, give or take, simply to look forward to loving and guiding the amazing new little person you're about to bring into the world. During that time, you're even described as "expecting."

Do you look forward to every day with such expectancy? You can. All you have to do is change your mind. Imagine what new opportunities and discoveries might be "born" to you on any given day! You will greatly increase your chances of making new discoveries when you get up out of bed each morning—*expecting* them to be there, whatever comes your way.

More and more, as you think and write your way through your DISCOVERY JOURNAL, your sense of expectancy will increase. Your positive expectations will propel you forward. And you will have a heightened awareness of the miracles disguised as coincidences that you encounter each day.

I can keep my sense of expectancy intact by making sure I do things like (i.e., really see the wonders of nature, feel gratitude for the simplest things—like breathing, be in the moment rather than be anxious about "tomorrow," etc.) . . .

_____

_____

_____

_____

_____

_____

2. Courage . . . Positively a "must-have" to be a great discoverer. Courage helps you through the obstacles you'll run into during the day. Some mornings you just wake up with the blues, if not downright depressed. Maybe your child is struggling to grow up. Or maybe you've just hit one too many bumps in a row and you don't feel so "positively you" that day. Those are the times to draw from the strength of your courage to get you through.

I'll have plenty of courage for the rough times when I do things like (i.e., unpack my self-doubt!, remind myself of former courageous acts, have realistic expectations, acknowledge that obstacles and hard times are opportunities in disguise, etc.) . . . _____

_____

_____

_____

_____

_____

3. Your Dreams . . . Remember *them?* We all have taken at least one detour on our way to making a dream come true. Dreams are vital to life's journey. With the vision of your dream clearly in your mind's eye, you can create doable goals or steps to lead you there.

Case in point—you are holding a dream come true. Because my dream in life has been to share with other women some of the tools I have acquired in my own often-frustrating struggle to believe in myself. And now the *Positively You!* DISCOVERY JOURNAL exists.

The lesson? *Dream big.* With all the positives you're packing for the journey, you'll realize your dreams sooner than you may think. *Someone* gets to write books, star in plays, plan their communities—why not you? Use this opportunity to begin to reconnect with your dreams and to redirect your path. Remember and write about long-held dreams and new ones too *The dreams I positively want to bring along on my life's journey include* (i.e., being debt-free, achieving a healthy weight once and for all, building my own business, writing a novel, finishing my education, etc.) . . . _____

_____

_____

_____

_____

4. Commitment . . . It goes hand in hand with making your dreams come true. I'm talking a no-matter-what-it-takes kind of inner resolve to stay the course. Not sure what true "commitment" looks like? That's not surprising. It seems we have fewer examples these days of true commitment, in everything from a higher rate of divorce to the changing trend away from career longevity with one company.

Look for and talk to people who are passionate and committed to what they do. Then factor what you learn along the way into your own unique brand of life commitment. I promise you, the stronger your commitment to make the "journey" in your DISCOVERY JOURNAL, the more meaningful the discoveries you'll make.

Really *committing* to your dream is about keeping it alive. Commitment is not a project; it's a process. And it's a mind-set— a passion—regardless the size of your dreams. *I'll have plenty of commitment for the journey as long as I do things like* (i.e., believe in myself, recommit to the journey every day, look for people who are examples of true commitment to encourage me along the way, etc.) . . . _____

_____

_____

_____

_____

_____

5. Energy . . . Do the words "sleep," "healthy diet," and "regular exercise" mean anything to you? How about the word "sanity"? Maintaining your physical energy makes an absolute world of difference in maintaining your mental, spiritual, and emotional *energy* for the journey. The greatest robber of all these things? Overcommitting and overscheduling. *Balance* is key to keeping your energy. And if I can do this, anybody can. *Some ways I can optimize my physical energy for the journey include* (i.e., prioritizing health in my daily schedule, going to bed 30 minutes earlier than usual, taking stretching and walking breaks from my work, reading instead of watching TV in bed (I find it so much more calming), cutting back on the caffeine and sugar, etc.) . . . _____

_____

_____

_____

_____

_____

6. Balance . . . It's key and definitely worth striving for! There's much debate among women as to whether or not balance truly is possible in our lives. I believe we can have it all . . . but not necessarily at the same time! One tool that's helped me immensely is to divide the areas of life into four parts—Work, Home, People, and Self. These are the four areas of life in which we strive for balance.

Pack plenty of "balance-mindedness" for the road ahead. *When it comes to the Work area of my life, I can bring more balance to my job and career by* (i.e., getting to work on time so I can head home on time, scheduling appointments wisely, not overcommitting to projects, making sure to schedule time for myself—even at work, etc.) . . . _____

_____

_____

_____

_____

When it comes to the Home area of my life, I can bring more balance to my relationship with my family by (i.e., cooking together, walking and talking together, being protective of time with my spouse, sharing household responsibilities, etc.) . . . _____

_____

_____

_____

_____

When it comes to the People area of my life, I can bring more balance to my relationships with friends and co-workers by (i.e., getting the toxic people out of my life, balancing the time I spend with relatives (remember those "distant" relatives!), making time to develop new friendships, putting myself in my friends' shoes, etc.) . . . _____

_____

_____

_____

_____

_____

And finally, when it comes to the Self area of my life, I can bring more balance to my physical, spiritual, and emotional relationship to myself by (i.e., exercising, devoting 15 minutes a day to prayer or meditation, scheduling some "play time" for myself each week, spending time thinking and writing in my DISCOVERY JOURNAL each day, etc.) . . .

_____

_____

_____

_____

_____

_____

7. Time for Yourself . . . **It's the number one thing women tend to leave behind!** I know we touched on this as it relates to "balance" above. But when you don't make time for yourself, you basically *deny* your worth as a person who has her own dreams, her own life, her own journey. I challenge you to celebrate yourself by making time for *you*.

I realize you may have forgotten what "time for yourself" is. But, trust me, such time can exist and you do have what it takes to *make* time for yourself. You'll need measured doses of it if you're going to make the most of your DISCOVERY JOURNAL!

(And, by the way, time for yourself means time for spiritual renewal and time for play—not extra time for work!) If you need proof of how taking time for yourself can renew your perspective, simply recall how stress just seems to melt away the minute you're heading out on vacation.

I can create time for myself by doing things like (i.e., meditating or praying daily, going to see a movie once a month, walking in my neighborhood at least three times a week, etc.) . . . _____

_____

_____

_____

_____

_____

8. Creativity . . . This journal is a good place to start, but it's **not intended to set limits on your own creative powers!** Need more room to write? Create your own companion DISCOVERY JOURNAL. There are no rules when it comes to using your imagination to create new ways to be *positively you.*

What's that? You don't think you're very creative? Think again. First, you can turn off that old tape that says you don't have a creative bone in your body. Then simply start brainstorming ideas. There's nothing like a renewed sense of creativity to provide a steady supply of fuel for the journey.

I can keep plenty of "positively me" creativity on hand by (i.e., trusting my intuition when I have the opportunity to be creative, experimenting with new creative outlets like interior design or painting or writing, looking at a difficult situation from a different perspective, etc.) . . . _____

_____

_____

_____

_____

_____

Be careful not to judge your ideas. Instead, be open to your creativity. It will bring you greater freedom and new possibilities for the journey.

9. Positive Attitude . . . **A positive attitude helps you rise above life's difficulties.** You can't always control the difficulties—things like when and where tough stuff happens and whom it effects. But you can control how you're going to view a given situation. You can choose to see through a negative lens or a positive one.

A positive attitude comes easier once you've unpacked the negative stuff. And keep in mind that just because a person has a positive attitude doesn't mean that person never has a negative thought or a problem. "Packing" a positive attitude simply is a smart way of dealing with problems. Bringing along a positive attitude does not mean you won't experience stress and strife. It just means you'll handle whatever life brings your way—in stride.

I can keep my positive attitude at an all-time high by making sure I (i.e., keep those negatives unpacked, get my

rest, maintain my balance, don't automatically jump to the worst
conclusion of a situation, etc.) . . . _____

_____

_____

_____

_____

Here's a tool often used in 12-step programs for helping maintain balance—it's called H.A.L.T. The letters stand for "hungry,"
"angry," "lonely," and "tired." When you let yourself get too
hungry, angry, lonely, or tired it can put a definite *halt* to your
positive attitude! Keeping those four things in check makes a
world of difference.

10. Positive People . . . **Bring along every positive person
you can find.** I know this can be a challenge. Sometimes it appears the cards are stacked against the positive people in the world.
But, hey! You're becoming more conscious of leaving behind
negativity, right? And you're committed to not letting negative
people influence your life. So now's the time to focus on drawing
close to *positive* friends and family who believe in you and encourage you to be the best you can be.

*I'll have plenty of positive people along for the journey
as long as I do things like* (i.e., build my relationships with
positive people, limit the time I spend watching negative people
on TV (it's bad for your psyche), refuse to participate in negative
conversations about others, etc.) . . . _____

_____

_____

_____

_____

_____

"What I do, I know." And now you know how empowering it is to be packed and ready to move on. Just look at all the positives you've packed for the journey:

- ✍ A Sense of Expectancy
- ✍ Courage
- ✍ Your Dreams
- ✍ Commitment
- ✍ Energy
- ✍ Balance
- ✍ Time for Yourself
- ✍ Creativity
- ✍ Positive Attitude
- ✍ Positive People

You are ready! Journey on . . .

My Own Journey:
How I Came to Believe in *Myself* Again

I want to give you a brief account of my life's journey—so far! I've gained valuable insights for my own journey by hearing about

Just a Note . . . Expect to encounter more of my trusty "road and driver" analogies up ahead. I can't help myself—my father was a used-car dealer! When I was younger, I discovered that just as cars can get out of alignment and become difficult to keep on course, so can people. I learned early the importance of things like balanced wheels, engine tune-ups, and keeping your hands on the steering wheel and your eyes on the road. *Lessons that have served me well.*

the travels of others. Maybe *my* story will give you some ideas about new things you'd like to try and things you'd like to avoid! Here goes.

I was born and raised in the West Texas town of Dumas. As the daughter of a used-car dealer dad and a hardworking mom, I had to become responsible for myself at an early age. I spent summers working in the maize fields. As a teenager, I was bucktoothed, overweight, and increasingly obsessed with creating the right exterior image to cover the insecurities and fears that made me ache on the inside.

Somewhere along the way I began to equate my own life with a car that needs tuning and balancing. As an adult, it didn't take me long to realize I wasn't driving a very reliable car. Too many things always felt out of balance. When I'd try to realign myself, I'd just run into more obstacles and be in greater need of repair. The imbalance in my life constantly pulled me in a direction I didn't want to go.

I attempted to compensate for the imbalance by trying to look good on the outside. I thought if I appeared to be "in control," then my life would be in control. Although my exterior "cleaned up nice," my inner "get-up-and-go" was in much need of attention. I lived with a chronic case of disappointment in myself. I longed to change my life, never realizing it was my thinking that needed an overhaul.

One day, I became so full of self-doubt and so overwhelmed by a sense of depression that I checked myself into a hospital. For days, I could barely talk to my family or my closest friends. I had hit bottom.

It was at that point I made a conscious decision to change my life—from the inside out. Determined to rid my life of the emptiness and despair I had tried so hard to hide with the "right" exterior image, I began to search my soul for the strength to slay my personal dragons.

Through facing the negative side of myself, I was able to tell my fears to hit the road—fears that, since early childhood, caused my inner engine to misfire. My positive side grew stronger as I "unpacked" negatives like the guilt, self-criticism, and fear of failure I talked about in the earlier unpacking exercise. I realized that throughout my life I had allowed all these negatives to steer me in the direction of postponing life instead of living it.

It was a time of reawakening and learning to believe in myself again. I began to find ways to make every moment in my life count. To embrace the things that matter most. And to reach out to others so that they too might discover their own potential for change.

As of the writing of this DISCOVERY JOURNAL, I'm still at it.

But I must tell you, you don't just wake up one day and decide, "I think I'll completely change my thinking today." It's an ongoing process that becomes a part of your life. I liken it to breathing awareness, where you catch yourself taking short shallow sips of air when you could be taking nice deep breaths.

Then came that incredibly fateful day in 1981, when my husband Richard and I took the risk of our lives. Our risk came in the form of a $600,000 loan to build BeautiControl Cosmetics, a company we dreamed would change the lives of thousands of women throughout America.

With eight employees and about 150 salespeople, we grew the business to a point where we were able to take our company public in 1986. The next year we were listed as one of the 100 fastest-growing small companies in America by *Business Week* magazine. Today, ours is the world's premier skin care and image company, with more than 60,000 women (and a growing number of men) working as BeautiControl Consultants and Directors on three continents!

We not only equip the women who join our company with the products and opportunity to sell, we also offer them real tools for personal transformation. That's a pretty valuable benefit when a salesperson's success is dependent on her motivation. But please know, I did not write *Positively You!* or this DISCOVERY JOURNAL to persuade you to go into cosmetic sales or to join our company.

I simply have this incredible drive to convince as many women as I can of the life-changing power that comes from believing in yourself. That's why I dreamed of writing books: to share my stories and those of other women I know who've learned to turn their lives around. How did we do it? It comes down to four keys:

1. We learned we didn't have to be subjugated to the negative attitudes or expectations of others.
2. We learned to let go of the burden of our pasts.
3. We learned that a meaningful life comes from what we give, not just what we receive. And . . .
4. We learned the incredible value of keeping our wheels balanced—"wheels" representing those four main areas of life (Work, Home, People, and Self), which you wrote about in the earlier exercise on "balance."

I believe with these four keys, you can accomplish anything you want. Advance in a career. Gain self-esteem. Develop deeper and more solid relationships. Or simply meet the everyday challenges of adult life.

My dream in life has been to share with other women some of the tools I've acquired along the way to believing in myself again. Today, I am living out my dream and it's the greatest feel-ing in the world. From here on, these pages are about *your* story and how you are turning *your* life around.

Are you postponing your dream? Start living it instead. Be-lieve me, you can do this. Positive change is within your power.

May you discover meaningful new ways to stay the course.

Learning

to Believe

in Yourself

Again

Specific Steps to
Help You Put "Today"
in Perspective

Please take this 10-second personal survey and answer two questions designed to help you see if you're happy about where you are going in your life's present journey. Answer each one as sincerely as you can. And be sure to write down the first yes-or-no answer that pops into your head so you won't overthink or rationalize your answers.

1. **If you were told you had just one year to live, would you continue to live your life exactly the way you are living it now?** *Absolutely* ("yes" or "no" will do) . . .

   _____

2. **Imagine that you are about to retire from your life's work and there is a testimonial dinner in your honor. Do you feel that the speakers that evening will be able to say the kinds of things about you that describe a woman who has become all she has dreamed of becoming?** *Actually* (again, a simple "yes" or "no") . . .

   _____

For me, these questions help put "today" in perspective.

That's all any of us really have is our *todays*. And even though each one of us has the power to orchestrate our own success, many of us live in a constant state of holding back. We never get around to "unpacking" procrastination. Instead of getting up to speed and being in balance with ourselves and the world around us, we chug along in the "comfort zone"—never experiencing the joy of taking the road less traveled.

Are you sure the road you're on will get you where you want to go?

What Do You Want Your Life to Be Like a Year from Now?

I don't know about you, but this kind of question always used to put me off. Then I realized it was because I had become well practiced at postponing my life instead of really living it.

For one, there was my fear of failure, of which I spoke earlier, along with the other negative baggage I had chosen to lug around. And even with those negatives weighing me down, I still could offer up glib answers about what I'd want my life to be like in one year. I just couldn't manage to fill in the "and here's what I'm going to *do* about it" part of the equation.

Wishful thinking is not change-your-life thinking.

Here's the kind of thinking I'm talking about. Let's say you've decided that a year from now you want to be able to speak basic conversational French. Great. Now ask yourself, "What am I going to *do* about it?" List specific actions you can take to reach your goal. For instance, enroll in a class at a local community college or university. Check out a tutorial audiotape from your neighborhood library. Join the local French Club. See a French film every once in a while—the kind without subtitles.

You get the idea. Follow your self-prescribed course of action and—voilà! At year's end, when someone asks you, "Parlez-vous Français?" you could answer "Bien sûr!"

I call that kind of thinking *action thinking*.

Only when I began to discover how to change my thinking process did I truly believe I could make changes in my life that would take me where I wanted to go—even within the period of one year.

And exactly how does one change one's thinking? In my case, it meant I had to ask myself, "What really drives me? What thoughts motivate me to take the actions that will get me off the wrong road and headed in the direction I want my life to go?"

Sometimes I have thought, *Who am I to think* I *can change?*

And what about you? This may be one question you just can't answer right now. You still may not be ready to change your life.

Maybe you just want your life to stay the way it is for now, That is not a crime! But if you really want to do something you've talked about for years and always postponed, you can change that. Now is the time to ask yourself the questions that will help you envision what your life can be and help you determine the course of action that will move you in that direction.

Tune-up Exercises

What do I want my life to be like a year from now? Remember, it's paper; you're not engraving stone. Maybe it will help you to start by jotting down some notes about what you don't want life to be like a year from now. Then try focusing on one significant change you'd like to work toward. Or maybe you'd rather set a specific one-year goal for each of the four main areas of life: Work, Home, People, and Self. All four areas need balance. *One year from now, I want my life to have* (i.e., **Work**—more organization; **Home**—more harmony; **People**—more positive friends; **Self**—more "me" time, etc.) . . . _____

_____

_____

_____

_____

_____

_____

_____

_____

_____

_____

_____

_____

_____

And here are the ways I can reach my one-year goal (i.e., **Work**—prioritize projects; **Home**—take more one-on-one time with family members; **People**—list what a negative friend costs me in terms of emotion, energy, and time; **Self**—cut back on my "activities," etc.) . . .

1. _____

_____

_____

_____

_____

_____

2. _____

_____

_____

_____

_____

_____

3. _____

_____

_____

_____

_____

_____

What do I want my life to be like *five* years from now?
Take the direction you established for your one-year answer and
develop it further. Dream as big as your imagination will allow.
Five years from now, I want my life to include (i.e.,
living a different lifestyle, more travel, more education, etc.) . . .

_____

_____

_____

_____

_____

_____

_____

_____

_____

_____

_____

_____

_____

_____

_____

_____

_____

_____

_____

_____

Here are three ways I can move toward my five-year goal (i.e., **change of lifestyle**—make a doable long-range plan/ simplify my life by moving to the country and/or working out of my home; **traveling more**—begin planning and saving to go on one or more trips to a fabulous destination; **learning more**— take steps to enroll in night college, etc.) . . .

1. _____

_____

_____

_____

_____

_____

2. _____

_____

_____

_____

_____

_____

3. _____

_____

_____

_____

_____

_____

_____

Am I on the right road to get there? *Actually,* ("I am" or "I am not" will suffice—answer according to where you are now) . . . _____*on the road that will take me where I want to be one year/five years from now.*

Whether you're on the right road or not, the important thing is you're more conscious of where you are right now. And you've discovered some specific actions you can take to keep on the course toward believing in yourself once more.

Finding

the Way,

Going the

Distance

How to Stop
Spinning Your Wheels
and Start
Changing Your Life

When I work out, I sometimes ride a stationary bike. It's the kind that lets you work your lower body by pedaling with your feet and work your upper body by moving the handlebars back and forth while you pedal.

I sit on that bicycle and really get my heart rate going. But for all the energy I expend, I actually go nowhere. Don't get me wrong. It's a great way to exercise indoors during stormy weather, but I'll take a long walk or a good run over riding in-place any day. There's just something to be said for getting outdoors and *going* somewhere. For me, it's simply more motivating to make time for exercise when I approach it as going out instead of working out!

There were times when my life was like a never-ending ride on a stationary bike. My actions revolved around maintaining my comfort zone. I turned "going through the motions" into a fine art—expending plenty of energy but never moving in the direction of my dreams.

I had created a risk-free existence for myself, one that was so routine, so familiar, I almost fooled myself into thinking I was really *living* my life.

Finally, I realized it was time to move forward.

Just a Note . . . Here's something to try next time you feel stuck in neutral. Maybe you wake up one day lost in the land of the blahs. When I find myself stopped in that place, that's my cue to *move*. Especially if my mind is feeling stagnant or stumped for a fresh idea to use in my work. Next time this happens to you, wake up your body with fresh air, exercise, healthy food, or loud music that gets you moving! Changing your thinking requires mind, soul, and body.

Signs Along the Way

My comfort zone became my own personal one-way "stuck spot." Despite all the preoccupation with my outward self, I grew even more insecure about my identity. I stayed on the wrong road for a tragically long period of time, locked in the same unsatisfying roles, maintaining my same old destructive habits.

I found out the hard way, you can't get on the right road in life until you learn *how* to get off the wrong one. What's more, it's important to figure out *why* you got on the wrong road in the first place. Otherwise, well, you know what happens. Someone gives you good directions to find the right road, but you still end up on the wrong one.

Have you noticed signs lately that indicate you may be on a wrong road? Maybe you're overstressed, easily angered, feeling overwhelmed, or you're unable to do things you've normally done with joy. Are you at a crossroads of one kind or another?

Don't stay stuck in neutral like I did for so long.

And don't let mistakes hold you back. Let's say you went on this incredibly healthy diet and you were so good for three whole weeks, but during one particularly stressful week you fell off the diet and felt like a failure. Listen, you *weren't* a failure! You lowered your calories. It was better for your body. You began a process. And all you have to do is recommit to that process.

A mistake is not a failure—it's an opportunity to get back on track. The same principle applies to you and your journey to being *positively you*. If you start thinking negatively or you get off track, that's okay. It's just a matter of mentally steering your thoughts in the direction that will get you back on your course of action.

You *will* regain the courage you seek to take control of your personal steering wheel once more. You *can* go the distance to *positively you*.

Put Yourself on the Map

Earlier you made some notes about what you want your life to be like a year from now, and five years from now. You've begun to establish your destination, or at least a more defined direction in which to move. Still, you may be frustrated to realize you once were quite close to being more positively you, but one wrong turn has taken you a considerable distance away from the life you dreamed of.

Or it's just as possible that you will be encouraged when the map reveals you are much closer to where you want to be than you even realized. Spend some time with the next three "Who am I?" and "Where am I going?" discovery questions and pinpoint your personal coordinates on the road map of life . . .

Who am I? Remember . . . first thoughts. Not your entire life story. What comes to mind? Your name? Your age? Your parents? Your children? Your work? Your hobbies? Your dreams? How do you define yourself? *I am . . .* _____

_____

_____

_____

_____

_____

_____

_____

_____

_____

_____

_____

Think about how you just defined yourself. Was it in terms of your "connections"? Is your identity so entwined with your relationships that you've lost touch with "you"? For instance, you may be "his wife," "her mom," and "my manager's assistant," and so on. As women, we simply tend to be consumed with our connections to other people because we're so relationship-oriented.

In professional development sessions with our company's new directors, it's always fascinating to hear them share their list of qualities. They describe themselves with words like "caring," "giving," and "generous." Their identity is totally about giving to others. I rarely hear them share things about themselves, like— "I'm willing. I'm attractive. I'm happy. People like to be with me. I'm entertaining. I'm funny."

I feel like saying, "Repeat after me: 'I am smart and creative and productive and who I am or who I can be is not limited by my relationships!' " We are so reared and so geared in our society; it's hard to imagine ourselves as more. Everything is so labeled it's hard for us to define who we *are*.

I want you to answer the question "Who am I?" again. Only this time, think about who you are besides just your "connections."

Reconnect—with you.

Who am I? *Come to think of it, I also am* (i.e., optimistic, moody, a strategic thinker, a dreamer, more assertive than I let on, etc.) . . . ───────────────────────

───

───

───

───

───

Where am I going? Be honest with yourself. Given the patterns and pieces of the puzzle that currently "drive" your life, where are you headed right now? In the direction of your dreams? Sidetracked? In circles? Write it the way you really feel about it. And don't forget to give yourself credit for the steps you are taking to get where you *want* to go. *Right now, I am going* (i.e., in circles, in the direction of my dreams, crazy, down the wrong path, etc.) . . . _____

_____

_____

_____

_____

_____

_____

_____

_____

_____

_____

_____

More "Finding Yourself" Exercises

Here's a list of my best qualities—the things I like most about myself. If you find this to be an awkward task, you are not alone. Sadly, many of us find it difficult at first to claim the positive qualities that make up our true essence. But, happily, once we begin to acknowledge what's good about who we are, we become energized to move with greater determination toward our dreams.

Where to begin? Start by listing a quality such as your sense of humor. Or maybe you have a great sense of direction. Or you have good "radar" when it comes to detecting negative people! You can even list physical traits if you like. Write down all the positives you can think of. *My best qualities include* (i.e., friendliness, open-mindedness, a sense of adventure, not being afraid of taking a risk on something or someone I believe in, etc.) . . . _____

_____

_____

_____

_____

_____

_____

_____

_____

_____

_____

And these are some of the dreams I've had for my life. Some of us live with constant reminders of unrealized dreams. Others of us simply block them out. Getting back in touch with your goals and dreams is important to the process of defining who you are and putting yourself on the map. *I have often dreamed* *of* (i.e., speaking French, being a dancer, a mom, a marine biologist, a world traveler, a gourmet chef) . . . _____

_____

_____

_____

_____

_____

_____

_____

_____

Somewhere along the way, something happened to my hopes and dreams. What made it so easy to put them aside? *These are some of the choices and decisions I've made along the way that have shifted my direction* (i.e., I chose to live more according to my "shoulds" and "oughts," I simply didn't feel capable, I chose to place certain obligations—like career or motherhood—before myself, etc.) . . . _____

_____

_____

_____

_____

_____

_____

_____

_____

_____

_____

_____

_____

   It's time to place some personal roadblocks to the dead-end roads I've been traveling . *I'm going to make some new choices and get some "new and improved" consequences, like* (i.e., resolving my conflicts with my husband so we can laugh together again, getting my debt under control so I can do the traveling I long for, making time to work out so I'll have the stamina to go back to school and finish my degree, etc.) . . .

_____

_____

_____

_____

_____

_____

_____

_____

_____

_____

_____

_____

Moving in the Direction of Your Dreams
Does Not Require Extreme Measures

Let's say you dreamed of an exciting career in finance, but you put your dream on hold. You chose to have a family, and when the twins were born, you decided to stay home. It's four years later. You love your life and those two little cuddly-wuddly kids, but now you'd like to steer back in the direction of that dream.

What are some of the changes you can start making *now*? How about getting a computer to work on at home? Why not go to the library to catch up on finance magazines and books. While you're still at home with the twins, you can begin the process of part-time work. Perhaps bookkeeping for a friend's business. Or tax consulting. Or maybe you'd like to try your hand at writing finance-related articles for a local business publication.

This is action thinking. You may not relate to the above situation, but you can use the same process in your own journey. Get a clear "vision" of where you want to go. Then simply take specific positive actions that will move you in the direction of your dreams.

You may ask, "Which comes first in this 'change your think-ing, change your life' process, anyway? Do you have to wait until you've changed your thinking *before* you can change your life?" *Absolutely not.*

When we take action we *transform* our thoughts. One aspect does not exist without the other. And putting your thoughts on the page certainly is a way of taking action. But don't fool yourself into thinking because you've written it down you've gotten it done. Let your actions fuel your thoughts.

For instance, want to start making time for physical exercise? Stop making so much time to watch TV or to keep a perfect house! Put up roadblocks. Place a sign on your television that insists you walk or work out first, then watch. And next time you head into a housecleaning frenzy, ask yourself what's going to move you closer to being *positively you*—a fit body and a sound mind or having all the product labels facing forward in your refrigerator?

Steering Instead of Fearing

Why does it take so long for some of us to overcome the fear that holds us in our comfort zones so we can, in turn, really change our lives? Why do we need to put on such a front for others? What intimidates us from turning the steering wheel and getting back on the right road?

We're *afraid* to believe in ourselves. Why? After so much time in our comfort zones, playing the various roles that we play, we literally lose touch with the best parts of ourselves. Deep down inside we know that if we're going to believe in ourselves again and act on that belief, we've got to be true to our skills, talents, and abilities.

Steering instead of fearing requires us to trust *our* own assessment more than that of others who may or may not have

our best interest at heart. If we're going to *start* believing in ourselves, we have to *stop* playing it safe, which means taking more risks. And that, I believe, is why we often resort to fearing instead of steering our lives in a better direction.

The very thought of "risk" makes us run.

If the thought of stripping off your comfortable old identity and showing who you really are makes you cringe, fear not. You are entitled to be yourself. And besides, everyone else has similar misgivings.

To learn to believe in yourself again—to change your direction—requires courage and commitment. Be confident in knowing your courage and commitment will grow in proportion to the personal discoveries you make.

A Few Practice Steering Exercises

When I daydream about the road I'd rather be traveling, I visualize myself doing all sorts of things. *Moving in the direction of my dreams, I can see myself* (i.e., working out three times a week, listening to my French tapes when I'm driving and doing housework, spending 30 minutes to an hour every day learning to use my new computer, etc.) . . . _____

_____

_____

_____

_____

_____

_____

_____

_____

_____

   I want to be present in the here and now, not just going through the motions. Instead of spinning my wheels in my daily routine, what specific ways can I stop and take pleasure in the ordinary moments of my days? *Even with things just as they are in my current circumstances, I can celebrate* (i.e., the place where I live as my own private sanctuary, my husband by seeing him as I saw him when we were dating, my "family" of co-workers—in spite of a difficult project, etc.) . . .

_____

_____

_____

_____

_____

_____

_____

_____

_____

_____

_____

What specific actions can I take to regain the self-confidence I've lost along the way? A specific action to regain self-confidence can be something as simple as taking time for *you*. Or maybe you could really use the listening ears and wise words of a mentor. You might be surprised how many women there are in your life who would count it an honor to encourage you in your journey. Don't be afraid to ask. *I will begin to believe in myself more and more as I* (i.e., make new discoveries in my journal, affirm my accomplishments no matter how small, turn my negative self-criticisms into positive affirmations, etc.) . . . _____

_____

_____

_____

_____

_____

_____

_____

_____

_____

And while we're on the subject of taking specific actions and steering instead of fearing, don't forget the very specific act of journalizing you're doing right now. It's a good sign you're steering in the right direction.

Check

Under the

Hood

Diagnosing
Negative Messages
That Put the Brakes
on Your Dreams

I recommend you tune in sometime to "Car Talk," National Public Radio's popular call-in program. You'll hear listeners nationwide call in to discuss their car woes, from the most obscure to the most common.

The two good-humored experts who host the show use ample doses of comedy to diagnose problems and prescribe solutions. Equally amusing, callers often attempt to imitate the strange range of noises their cars produce, in hopes that "Click" or his brother "Clack" will recognize the symptom and diagnose the problem right there on the air.

I'll never forget my reaction the first time I happened onto this program.

If only we were as attuned to the sounds coming from our "*inner* engines!" I laughed to myself. Just think, at the first sign of a negative message like "I am so stupid," or "I'll *never* make my dream come true," you'd refer to your owner's manual for help. Then you'd recognize that "clog"—or negative script—in your inner engine and you'd do something about it.

You'd make a few adjustments with your "positively you attitude" and you'd be on your merry way. You wouldn't think twice about that course of action. And if you weren't up to playing the role of mechanic, you'd seek help or advice from a caring friend, minister, family member, or professional counselor.

In the same conscientious way you take care of your mode of transportation, you would take care of the way you think. You'd never ignore a thought or a behavior that could slow you down in life.

You *can* learn to recognize and let go of the negative messages masked by "sounds" and scripts you've simply grown accustomed to hearing inside your head. And once you learn to pinpoint those inner negatives for the energy "leaks" and power "clogs" they really are, getting rid of them is a piece of cake!

True inner listening takes practice. One of the most valuable tools I use to sharpen my inner listening skills has to do with practicing my "inner *seeing*" skills.

Seeing Is Believing

I'm a big believer in the power of visualization. When I have a clear picture in my mind of me actually living out a particular dream or achieving a personal goal, it's as though I suddenly have bionic ears. My inner visualization of where I'm headed is so strong it sets off an alarm at the first rattle or squeak of negativity.

It took me several years in the school of hard knocks, but I finally learned exactly what to do when a negative message tries to clog up the lines in my inner engine. What do I do? I stop in mid-negativity. I acknowledge it for what it is—a negative message from the past and *not* my present truth. Then I get my eyes back on the road.

When I hold my focus on where I want to go, the negative messages of the past can no longer hold me back! My positive vision for the future is what gives me the strength to let go of my negative past. And that act of letting go enables me to "be" in the present and keep moving toward the future of my dreams. One step at a time.

I think of our minds as sometimes being in a similar state of confinement as those beautiful sleek dolphins swimming in those smaller-than-life water tanks at amusement parks. That's why visualization is so liberating. It allows us to imagine ourselves leaping and speeding our way in a glimmering blue ocean of possibilities.

As we develop this kind of mental "imaging" ability, we test the waters of our dreams. We can visualize ourselves really living our dreams. The power of our vision enables us to see who we truly are and what we truly can be. And because seeing is believing, our belief in ourselves is renewed.

Through our visualization, we believe we can, and so we do! Another dream becomes a reality. It happens every day.

I learned to make it happen for me. And I know women around the world who have learned to believe in themselves and in their dreams once more. They practice the art of looking and listening for those clogs in their inner engines. And by unlearning the past and visualizing a new future, they reinvent themselves.

Guess what? *Your turn.*

Just a Note . . . Sometimes, especially if you've been avoiding it for years, the process of "looking back" can cause you to look down. This is a friendly reminder to be sure to look up! Oh, and watch where you're going too. Be protective of this time for yourself. This kind of journey requires your *presence*. You'll want to conserve the energy you might ordinarily give to other activities so you'll stay energized to write and stay positive.

Remember the Time . . . ?

I want you to try a visualization technique that employs the simple act of *remembering*.

Remember a moment when you felt at your absolute best. It doesn't have to be a life-changing moment. It could be a simple stopping-to-smell-the-roses moment, like when you took a long walk with your child and felt that all was well with the world. It could be when you were exercising regularly and felt so alive and energized. Or it could be the way you felt when you fixed a problem at work and felt so alive and up to the challenges of your job.

Go ahead. Write about one of those "at your best" feelings.

I remember feeling at my best when I . . . _____

_____

_____

_____

_____

_____

_____

_____

_____

_____

_____

Have that image or visualization locked into your mind's eye? Good. Okay, there you are. You can see yourself at a real moment in time when you felt you were at your best. Now ask yourself, **Why is it I do not strive ceaselessly to have such moments in my life as often as possible?!**

Think of it this way: Do you keep your car running at its best? Your household? Your outer appearance? Okay. So, what about your inner engine? Your true self. The way you feel about *you* right now. Do you feel "at your best"? If the answer is "no," try to identify some of the negatives that may clog your inner engine and stop you in your tracks.

As I learn to let go of these negative messages from the past, they'll no longer have the power to hold me back. They include thoughts like (i.e., I'm unworthy, I'm unlovable, I'm unable, I'm inadequate, I'm slow, etc.) . . . ——

_____

_____

_____

_____

_____

_____

_____

_____

_____

_____

_____

What are some ways you can hold onto the power of that "at-your-best" visualization and use it to begin a lifelong practice of re-creating such moments in your life? In other words, what are some ways you can turn the *memory* of that feeling of positive energy into an ongoing mental photograph of you at your best? It can serve as visual representation of the ideal "you."

You then can harness the power of that visualization and hold it up in the front of your mind as you make choices and take action in the course of each day. Your choices can include choosing *not* to listen to the negative messages of the past. Your actions can include letting go of the negative messages or beliefs about yourself, and, instead, holding onto the positive visualization or image of yourself.

Think of your visualization like a giant flash card, always ready to be held up for review. Then, hold up that at-your-best mental image and move in that direction.

The inner conversation you have with yourself might sound something like "Okay, I've got the image planted firmly in my mind. This is the 'me' I'm going for. Not the sad me. Or the depressed me. Or the 'holding back' me. I want the 'positively' me!"

And off you go. *I will begin to re-create "at-my-best" moments when I use the power of my visualization* (i.e., to start the new business I've always wanted to start, to begin a lifelong fitness plan, to get my financial affairs in order, to experience loving relationships, etc.) . . . _____

_____

_____

_____

_____

_____

_____

_____

_____

_____

Regarding History and the Force of Habit

Before we delve further back in our memory banks to childhood days, I want to make it clear that this process is *not* about blaming our problems on our parents. Blaming our present behavior on someone else does not bring us any closer to believing in ourselves again or to realizing our dreams.

Ultimately, we are responsible for *who* we become. Period. This is not to say that many of us were not hurt emotionally or even physically in our pasts. But we're here, after all, to discover answers, not to find scapegoats. At the same time, I do not subscribe to the theory that one can just ignore the past or simply up and decide to turn over a new leaf.

Only with the insight of knowing how we arrived at our present road in life can we take measures to change our direction. That insight is key to becoming *positively you*. And that's why we must face our personal histories and acknowledge those negative feelings from our past. We've held onto them for so long that we allow them to govern our lives to this very day.

Think about that for a moment.

All our feelings of guilt, anxiety, fear, self-pity, and lack of self-esteem were learned from long-ago, obsolete experiences— yet we still hold onto them. In fact, many of our attitudes toward ourselves may not have changed since we were very young.

Here's an example that almost all of us can identify with.

Somewhere in our childhood was the message that failure is the dreaded enemy. We received the message in various ways that it was wrong to fail. It wasn't meant as a malicious lesson, of course, but many of us created a life for ourselves based on that message. Instead of really going for what we wanted, we created a safer life. A safety zone. We made a lot of "safe" decisions and formed all sorts of self-protective beliefs to reinforce the fact that we shouldn't do this or that in order to avoid the possibility of failure.

This "failure factor" resonates for many women and men I know. Perhaps it resonates for you. Maybe you feel like you've been keeping in the far right lane on the highway to your dreams, refusing to get up to even the minimum speed limit. Is your fear of failure causing you to do just that? If so, check under the hood and try to locate some specific ways you've learned to put the brakes on your own dreams.

When I stop and think about it, I've created my own safety zone. Avoiding the risk of failure, I tend to (i.e., send the most creative side of myself underground, use emotions of the past to deal with people in the present, assume that I am inadequate instead of capable, etc.) . . . _____

_____

_____

_____

_____

_____

_____

_____

_____

_____

No wonder we feel clogged and sluggish in the pursuit of our dreams! To understand why we respond to situations the way we do requires that we understand our personal histories.

But how does one actually go about understanding his or her

history? For me, the understanding came with becoming more aware, more conscious, of the long list of negative messages I'd managed to pick up and hold onto along the way from childhood to adulthood.

These messages—I'd convinced myself—were "my" messages, my story, my truth. When in fact, they'd been projected on my mind and memory for so long that I'd lost sight of my own truth. It was *my* story that I needed to be about the business of "writing"—simply by being *positively me.*

What a relief to know that just as we learn certain negative beliefs about ourselves as growing children, it is just as possible to *unlearn* them as growing adults.

Held Over Due to Popular Demand . . .

We all know what it's like to see a film so moving, so powerful, that we carry its images and meaning, its dialogue—even its soundtrack—around in our heads for days. It's almost like the movie's story and images provide us with a fresh lens through which to view our own lives and our own possibilities.

Now, imagine the "movie" of your own life story—your childhood, to be more specific—playing an endless engagement on the big screen of your mind. The images may be loving and sweet. They may be turbulent and disturbing. The dialogue may be filled with positive messages or negative ones.

Whether you realize it or not, the images and messages of that movie either propel you forward to make your dreams come true, or the power of that long-playing movie holds you in a hypnotic state that keeps you from getting where you want to go in life.

Can't shake the negative images and messages of the old home movies in your mind? No wonder! Remember, most of our attitudes about ourselves haven't changed since our formative years.

This calls for an "awakening" exercise.

I want you to play "movie critic" for a moment. First off, write a synopsis of the movie of your childhood years. Do it in the space provided here or write it in a separate notebook. Give your movie a title if you like. And a location. You can even rate it if you want. Be sure to include as many insights or "clues" to your negative beliefs as you can. Acknowledge your positive beliefs, too, while you're at it.

The more you write, you may find the more there is to *unlearn*! Take as much time and space as you need. *My childhood movie starts out with me* (i.e., crying alone in my room, giggling endlessly while my parents tickle me, running scared up to the attic and looking for a place to hide, playing outside with friends, etc.) . . . _____

_____

_____

_____

_____

_____

_____

_____

_____

_____

_____

_____

_____

_____

_____

_____

_____

_____

_____

_____

_____

_____

_____

_____

_____

_____

"Rewind and play" the film over in your mind. Really study as you read the movie of your childhood years. Dissect it. Analyze it. Look at it with both eyes open. Observe the recurring patterns of negative feelings and choices you made that were not really "you."

Case in point: It would be easy to watch a movie of *my* childhood years and say that nothing was my fault—that I should have seen what was happening around me and realized it had nothing to do with my own self-esteem. But like most children, I internalized my family problems. I thought it was my fault in some way that things weren't smooth. And so I came to the conclusion I was not lovable and unconsciously decided that what I had to do to get love was *to be recognized*. To compensate for my childhood feelings that I was unworthy, I started playing all sorts of "roles" that weren't really me.

What roles did you play in the movie of your childhood? Did you become your school's human *doing* instead of human *being*? That's what I did. Or maybe you took on the role of "caregiver" at a very early age. Review your movie again and document the roles you played then. *In the movie of my childhood, I play the part of* (i.e., the child who only appeared to be happy, the child who took care of the parent, the child who craved praise and attention, the rebel child, the spoiled brat, etc.) . . . _____

_____

_____

_____

_____

_____

_____

_____

_____

_____

_____

_____

With your childhood roles fresh on your mind, write down the roles you still play as an adult. The similarities may astound you. *Today I'm still playing the role of* (i.e., human doing, caregiver to all, the rebel, the spoiled brat, etc.) . . .

_____

_____

_____

_____

_____

_____

_____

_____

_____

_____

_____

_____

_____

_____

Letting Go of "Then."
Taking Hold of "Now."

By letting go of painful past attitudes, we can look at ourselves in a different way. We can come alive again. We are empowered to make changes in our future because we have looked into the past. We have learned to care enough about ourselves to pay closer attention to the things that slow us down.

It many respects it's true that a car is a lot like a person. Neither one is designed to be continuously "driven" without periodically checking under the hood, so to speak. And what did we find? Life constantly calls us to change! We *are* up to the challenge.

The acts of looking back and of looking forward help us to see ourselves more clearly and to believe in ourselves once more. I hope these exercises have helped you pinpoint the source of your doubts and fears, and that you are picking up speed on your way to making your dreams come true.

In the

Driver's Seat

Power Steering
Your Way Back
to Your Strengths

Up to this point, perhaps you've spent your life tuned in to too many negative messages. If so, no doubt you're "well-rehearsed" at playing roles that often serve only to focus your energy on suppressing what you *believe* to be your weaknesses.

It's time to turn your attention to your greatest strengths instead. The *real you* is the most rewarding role you'll ever play. Maybe you've grown so accustomed to playing roles, hiding behind masks, that you're having a little trouble imagining what life would be like without them.

Let me clarify something. There's nothing inherently wrong with adopting different roles in life. Just as we change hats or shoes for different occasions and activities, we often shift into any one of a variety of roles to manage relationships and situations more effectively.

The challenge comes when you spend more time and energy "acting the part" than you devote to finding out who you really are, what you actually want and what you truly are capable of becoming.

You may think the roles you play make you appear as though you're coping more successfully with life. However, so much emphasis on roles can lead to unhappiness. That means, without realizing it, millions of busy role-playing women (and men) are working very hard at *avoiding* happiness.

Imagine that. The force of habit is so gradual and so powerful we literally get in the habit of unhappiness. It's a sad commentary, but thankfully, it's not a life sentence. Take heart. You *can* break the habit of unhappiness and reconnect with your strengths.

Stop the Car—I Want to Get Out!

Feel like you've fallen asleep at the wheel? Realize that you've been letting your roles do the driving? If so, it's time for an awakening. Pull off to the side of the road, roll down the windows, and breathe in the fresh air of awareness.

You're just around the corner from becoming more conscious of how the negative messages of your past "write" the scripts for the roles you play today. That "role awareness" will empower you to grab hold of the wheel and take charge of your life. At that point of self-realization, you can get yourself off the road that leads away from happiness and back on the road to your dreams.

Here's another way to think of yourself and the roles you've taken on. Picture the root cause of your problems in life as a sort of "Grand Canyon" of space you've allowed into your thinking. That vast expanse separates the parts of yourself that you *privately* submerge—and the roles you *publicly* display.

Now, imagine yourself with all your roles and masks and scripts gathered around you there in your "comfort zone." You gaze longingly across the distance to where the real you patiently waits on the other side.

How in the world can you get back to being *positively you?*

You *can* build a bridge. You *can* take one step at a time.

The Power of Roles

Understanding the power of roles is a positive step toward bridging that gap between the public parts we play and the best parts of ourselves that we privately hold back.

Pretend the upcoming "role call" list is a kind of mirror. This "mirror" will reflect aspects of yourself that ordinary mirrors fail to reveal. I see parts of myself in nearly all of the roles listed. You'll probably see yourself in more than one role too.

What I want you to notice is how many good qualities there are in these roles. You'll find descriptions of women who are driven to excellence and those who are blessed with compassion. You'll also find that the *hidden power* of roles lies in the way it becomes easy to distort those wonderful qualities and use them as self-protective shields.

Our strengths and our liabilities help create the roles we play. Identify the roles you play so you can pinpoint your positive traits and your negative ones. With that knowledge, you can begin to harness the power of the *positive* traits from your various roles to grab hold of the wheel and leave those *negative* ones in the dust.

Role Call

The Perfectionist. She's hard to please, no matter what she's accomplished. She has difficulty congratulating herself. She's preoccupied by what she "should" be doing and forgets to ask herself what she wants or needs. She's lost touch with the spontaneous little girl inside. It's hard for her to play or do something that could bring her joy.

At work, the Perfectionist is the one who delivers outstanding products and services. And she's a great leader as long as she doesn't set standards that no one else can reach. She puts tremendous pressure on herself and sometimes on others. The Perfectionist has a need for order and routine and there's an inner pressure to use every minute productively. As a result, she finds it difficult to relax, enjoy life, or easily accept what comes her way. *What happened to make her feel this way?*

The Perfectionist's message from the past tells her she wasn't good enough. Now she's trying to prove through her perfection that she's not only good enough, but that she's the best.

Do you sometimes play the role of the Perfectionist? If so, how? (Note: Even if you don't think a particular role description applies to you, consider each one carefully. You may not be a Perfectionist in a big way and yet there may be one area of your life where trying to be perfect is actually holding you back.) *Some of the ways I play the Perfectionist include* (i.e., my nonstop work habits, the way I "run" my children's lives, my obsession with having a "perfect" appearance, etc.) . . . ————————————————————

————————————————————————————————————

————————————————————————————————————

————————————————————————————————————

————————————————————————————————————

If the role of Perfectionist is a little too familiar, stop and think about how you can take the positive qualities of that role and put them to better use. *Here are some ways I can rechannel my drive to do more and to do it better* (i.e., BREATHE!, develop a relaxed human-being approach with my co-workers, get better at letting go of my need to control, learn to celebrate my natural appearance, etc.) . . . ————————————————

————————————————————————————————————

————————————————————————————————————

————————————————————————————————————

————————————————————————————————————

Take it from me—an experienced Perfectionist!—the key word here is "relax." And keep in mind that word "balance" too. There always is a reasonable *degree* of what is acceptable. Do that and you'll be happier.

The Caged Spirit. She possesses the great quality of humility. The problem is that she hasn't developed enough courage to stand up for herself. She has yet to develop the inner strength to truly believe her opinions are important. People tend to walk over her or use her. As a result, she may bury her own desires and hopes for the future. And as time goes on, she may become more self-conscious and vulnerable, or angry and resentful, causing her to remain inside the small space of her cage, where she feels safe. *What was her message?*

The Caged Spirit's message from the past tells her she wasn't good enough. Gee, wasn't that the negative message for the Perfectionist?! True. But there are as many different ways to respond to the same message as there are different individuals.

The Perfectionist tries to prove that she's more than good enough and doing it better than anyone. The Caged Spirit tries to prove that she's *enough* by never rocking the boat and always agreeing. The Perfectionist tries to prove *wrong* the message of "not enough," where the Caged Spirit tries (whether she realizes it or not) to prove the message "not enough" was *right.*

Do you play the role of the Caged Spirit? If so, be honest with yourself and write down some of the ways you try to live up to the "I'm not enough" message. *Some of the ways I play the Caged Spirit include* (i.e., the way I keep my thoughts and opinions to myself, the way I tend to take on more than my share of responsibilities, the way I avoid risk by staying in my comfort zone, etc.) . . . _____

_____

_____

_____

_____

_____

_____

_____

    If the role of the Caged Spirit hits a little too close to home, be kind to yourself and focus on how you can take the positive qualities of that role and put them to better use. *Here are some ways I can refocus my sense of humility to give new spirit to my life's direction* (i.e., graciously accept praise that comes my way, propose more sharing of responsibilities, give myself the gift of doing something I've always wanted to do but was afraid to try, etc.) . . . _____

_____

_____

_____

_____

_____

_____

The Saint. She's always accommodating others. To her credit, the Saint often is a good listener. She's compassionate and cares about others' needs. She above all really desires the best for others. In fact, she's created a life for herself in which her own needs are defined by how she serves and gives to others.

    Unfortunately, the Saint defines herself *only* through how others define her. She wants to be everyone's best friend and she's all too often disappointed when that doesn't happen. What makes this role even more difficult is that the Saint believes she's somehow responsible if another person doesn't like her. *What happened to make her feel this way?*

The Saint's message from the past is that she probably wasn't worth much if she didn't give of herself. Once again, it's another way of saying "not enough."

Do you sometimes play the role of the Saint? Then adjust your halo and grab your pen. Make some "confessional" notes here of the saintly ways you strive to prove that "not enough" message wrong. Come on now. Tell the truth. *Some of the ways I play the role of the Saint include* (i.e., giving and giving of myself to everything and everyone until I'm empty, spending too much time listening to others' problems and worrying how to "solve" them, etc.) . . . _____

_____

_____

_____

_____

_____

Okay now, set your halo off to the side for a minute. Envision those wonderful qualities of yours—caring, compassion, and being a good listener. I want you to write down some of the ways you can use those positive traits to bring more *balance* to your life. *Here are some caring ways I can move back into the driver's seat in life* (i.e., stop overscheduling myself to take care of others, plan time to do some of my favorite things, realize I'm not God and it's not my responsibility to "fix" everyone's problems, etc.) . . . _____

_____

_____

_____

_____

There's absolutely nothing sinful or selfish about being true to yourself and taking care of "you." The more caring, compassionate, and nurturing you are to yourself, the better you'll be at playing the role of Saint to others *sometimes* but also to yourself!

The Performer. She can't imagine being loved just for who she is. That's why the Performer focuses her attention on earning the kind of status that will guarantee others' admiration. She gives such a good "performance" that she is respected by most everyone she meets. She is likely to be a high achiever who can present an appearance of optimism and well-being.

The Performer thinks she must be loved for her achievements or by entertaining those around her. As a result, this person is fun to be around because she keeps things lively. But depending primarily on achievement for her happiness may backfire on the Performer. *What message did she receive?*

The Performer's message from the past is that she must perform, or fail to be acknowledged. That's why she feels responsible for "carrying" the dinner party or for just making people laugh.

Are you well rehearsed at playing the role of the Performer? We can all use a good sense of humor and the ability to have fun and be witty, but if the Performer role is driving your life, that means you've come to believe you are loved because of your performance and not just because you exist. Write down some of the ways you hide behind your drive to perform. *I get carried away playing the role of the Performer* (i.e., when I think I must speak at every meeting even when I'm exhausted, when I feel like I have to be "on," when I think people only like me because I'm witty and entertaining, etc.) . . . _____

_____

_____

_____

_____

_____

Now consider some of the ways you can use those wonderful qualities of optimism, humor, and the ability to achieve great things to head your life in a more positive direction. *I can more easily perform the role of "positively me"* (i.e., when I know I'm capable without having to "prove" it to others, when I relax and enjoy others as much as my own entertainment, when I celebrate the other talents I possess more than being the center of attention, etc.) . . . _____

_____

_____

_____

_____

_____

Bravo. From one Performer to another, I assure you that getting those thoughts on the page is quite an achievement in itself. Can you feel it? You're easing into the role of "you." A star is born.

The Pretty Woman. She's obsessed with her physical appearance, regardless of her talents or intelligence. Her life revolves around striving for physical beauty. Her self-worth depends on it. Still, the Pretty Woman is usually one we admire because she *appears* to be in control. She's always "pulled together." But as pretty as she may be, she often is focused on her flaws and not on her attributes. *What message did she receive?*

The Pretty Woman's message from the past is that girls/ women have to be pretty to be loved and accepted. In other words, you're "not enough" if you're not pretty.

Do you play the role of the Pretty Woman? There's nothing inherently wrong with being pretty or with caring about your appearance. I know from my own experience as a woman and from working with women that we want to be attractive, and society expects us to be so; yet we often believe we fall short because we compare ourselves to unrealistic standards.

The key here is: Do you judge your joy by your appearance?

Write down some of the ways you lose yourself playing the role of the Pretty Woman. *I play the Pretty Woman when* (i.e., I read fashion magazines, I compare myself to the models on the pages, I constantly think about something "new" to do to myself to improve my image, I can't relax unless I'm wearing makeup, etc.) . . . _____

_____

_____

_____

_____

_____

Okay. You've pretty much perfected the fine art of appearing to be in control, so stop worrying about that. With the confidence that comes from knowing how to look your best on the outside, now write about some of the ways you can use that positive energy to play up your inner attributes. *Here are some of the ways I can overcome my obsession with playing the role of the Pretty Woman* (i.e., I can remind myself that the thin eighteen-year-old models are retouched and are not reality, I can celebrate the health of my body and stop focusing on a few flaws, I can give myself permission to run errands sans makeup, etc.) . . .

_____

_____

_____

_____

_____

And, remember, when you go without your makeup *never* apologize for how you look. Men never do that, do they? Celebrate yourself!

The Crisis Queen. She "can't get no satisfaction." Fact is, she usually doesn't want any. Crisis and conflict make her feel normal. She probably experienced much conflict in her childhood, so peace and harmony actually feel uncomfortable. And since the Crisis Queen is usually *looking* for a crisis—if there isn't one, she'll create it! *What happened to cause her to behave this way?*

The Crisis Queen's message from the past is that she was not heard. Interestingly enough, we humans will actually create conflict to bring others closer to us or to be heard. Think about it—the squeaky wheel gets the grease.

Fess up. Do you play the role of the Crisis Queen? Look, just like with all the other roles listed here, the Crisis Queen is neither good nor bad. Remember, we choose each role subconsciously as a way to prove our messages from the past right or wrong. In a subconscious way, when we don't know how to ask for what we need, we will create conflict to get our needs met—just like a child who wants negative attention rather than no attention at all.

If you do sometimes play the Crisis Queen, writing about it does not have to be a crisis! *Honestly, the ways I play the Crisis Queen include* (i.e., I create a crisis at work so others will come to my aid, I create conflict instead of asking for what I need, I confront even the tiniest issue, etc.) . . . _____

_____

_____

_____

_____

All of us play this role from time to time. But if you think you might be playing Crisis Queen more often than you'd like, ask yourself what you get out of this behavior and whether there is a better way to get your needs fulfilled. *I can use my attention-getting skills in a more positive way by* (i.e., asking for help or sharing my needs, sharing my feelings and asking to be heard, breathing and realizing that each and every issue is just part of life, etc.) . . . _____

_____

_____

_____

_____

_____

Good for you. You *can* be heard, nurtured, and close to people without creating conflict.

The Blamer. She goes through each day of her life figuring out a new way in which she is not appreciated. Her emotional life basically consists of complaints about her own misfortunes. She finds it easier to groan about her situation than to change it. She always has an excuse for why she can't change. And she tends to blame everything or everyone for her circumstances. *What negative childhood message did she receive?*

The Blamer's negative message from the past is that she has no control. Yet another way of saying "not enough." Another role for proving that message wrong or right. Perhaps the Blamer witnessed an important person in her life not taking responsibility for his or her own problems. Maybe she saw her mother blame her father for their problems. Or she may have grown up hearing her father blame the world for his lack of financial success. Whatever happened, she found it easier in life to complain about a problem than to take action to fix it. She kept herself a victim.

Each of us plays the "blame game" from time to time, but constantly looking outside ourselves to hand off responsibility can lead to a lonely and unhappy life. Blamers often see themselves as helpless. Make note of some of the ways *you* play the Blamer. *I realize I play the role of the Blamer when* (i.e., I invest a lot of energy complaining instead of solving a problem, I blame my unhappiness on my husband or on my childhood, I make excuses about negative situations instead of using my capabilities to change things, etc.) . . . _____

_____

_____

_____

_____

_____

As you read back over the notes you just made, what strikes you about what you're getting out of this behavior? Does blaming really get you anywhere? Placing blame simply is an excuse to which many people cling to justify a "victim" position.

I am convinced that happiness is an active choice. Each of us has what it takes to stop placing blame and start laying claim to the happiness that can be ours. Make some notes here about specific steps you can take to move in that direction. *I can stop playing the role of the Blamer by* (i.e., looking for ways to solve a problem instead of complaining about it, catching myself when I make excuses and changing my words, realizing that "being happy" is my choice and responsibility, etc.) . . . _____

_____

_____

_____

_____

_____

Ever notice how people with physical impairments usually are not Blamers? They are grateful for what they have rather than focusing on what they don't have.

The Competitor. Whatever someone is doing well, the Competitor wants to do it better. She's great at taking risks and trying new things, but she has difficulty enjoying her own success. She's usually comparing herself with someone else. She has a hard time celebrating the success of others too because she feels inadequate. *What was the message she received?*

The Competitor's negative message from the past is "to be valued, you must be the best." It's hard to relax with the Competitor around because she makes almost everything a contest to be won or lost. She has difficulty enjoying "the game" because she is so determined to do it better or win next time that she finds it hard to stay in the present.

Sound like someone you know? Write down some of the ways playing the Competitor is keeping you from being *positively you. I play the role of the Competitor when* (i.e., I have difficulty enjoying a simple sports game because winning is so important, someone else succeeds at something and it's hard to celebrate because I'm focused on how I can accomplish more, etc.) . . . _____

_____

_____

_____

_____

_____

_____

While all of us can enjoy competition, we also can enjoy the *process* and let go of the *outcome*. Being present to enjoy the actual "game" and not just be consumed with the outcome is an important message for the Competitor.

Now list some ways you can make more positive use of that competitive spirit on your journey to a more positive *you*. *Ways I can rechannel my drive and ambition include* (i.e., choosing to be my coworkers' number one fan when they succeed, celebrating my personal successes—the little ones and the big ones, ceasing to compare myself to unrealistic standards, etc.) . . . _____

_____

_____

_____

_____

That message "to be valued, you must be the best" is but one more "I'm not enough" mantra . . .

The Procrastinator. She talks about what she's going to do, but delays taking the action to achieve what she's talking about. Usually, procrastination is about fear or fear of failure. In other words, I can talk all I want about something I'd like to accomplish, but if I don't do it, I *can't* fail! *What was the Procrastinator's message?*

The Procrastinator's negative message from the past is

probably twofold: "Don't fail" and "mistakes are failures." In other words, you're "not of value" if you make mistakes. And the easy way to not make a mistake is to avoid action.

"Me? Avoid action?!" you say? Hey, the role of the Procrastinator hits home with us all at some point. When you think of the ways you procrastinate in life, what are some of the first things that pop into your mind? *Some of the ways I've perfected the role of the Procrastinator include* (i.e., spending too much time talking about my projects at work when I could be accomplishing them, postponing the most important talks until something erupts, the way I delay my lifelong dream for fear of failure, etc.) . . . _____

_____

_____

_____

_____

If you're a Procrastinator, make a commitment to yourself to write out a plan with deadlines. Even if some of the deadlines aren't met, you'll realize that's not a sign of failure and then continue on to the next step. *These are just some of the ways I can take action in my life instead of postponing it* (i.e., shorten meetings at work and increase the "action sessions," stop waiting for "the right moment" to happen with my relationships and start discussing what's in my heart, make attainable goals toward realizing my lifelong dream, etc.) . . . _____

_____

_____

_____

_____

_____

_____

_____

_____

The Busy Doing. She keeps herself so busy that she doesn't have to feel or think about her own needs. And with so much on her plate, she never has to really develop any one personal quality. For example, the way her preoccupation with "doing" prevents her from exploring her creativity or stops her from paying more attention to things of a spiritual nature. *What negative message from the past has she been busy proving right?*

The Busy Doing received the message that her worth is related to doing and doing more. The feeling that you've got to do more and more means only one thing: What you're really feeling is that you are "not enough."

Are you so busy playing the role of the Busy Doing you've lost touch with your true desires and needs? Slow down then. Un-busy yourself and take a serious look at just what it is you're so busy doing. *The ways I play the role of the Busy Doing include* (i.e., always cleaning and feeling pressured about doing it all at once, doing two or three things at the same time until I'm not doing anything well, the way I never quite get going on my own dreams and desires because I'm "too busy," etc.) . . .

_____

_____

_____

_____

_____

As women, we often can take on too much. I believe any woman can do anything she desires, but not all at the same time. Spend a few minutes here writing about what that means to you. *Ways I can be a better-balanced Busy Doing woman include* (i.e., learning some breathing or relaxing techniques, making a list and doing *only* what's on the list, scheduling some time away from my "busyness" to develop my life dreams and desires, etc.) . . . _____

_____

_____

_____

_____

Here's a thought: To get out of the habit of playing The Busy Doing, take an occasional five-minute "do-nothing" break and just "be."

The Must Be. She *must* be right. We all know this woman. She's uncomfortable when someone is telling a shared experience and they mention a detail she thinks is incorrect. The Must Be interrupts the conversation and makes the correction. Am I right?!

It's like when my husband Richard shares a story about us with friends and says, "About nine years ago so and so, and such and such." And I interrupt and say, "No, honey. It was nine and *a half* years ago . . ." You get the picture. Of course, it doesn't matter whether it was nine or nine and a half years ago. That detail has no bearing on the story. *So, what is little Miss Must Be's message from the past?*

The Must Be tuned into the message that "to be valued, you must be right." It's a lot like the message of the Competitor, who, to be valued, "must be the best." The Must Be learned that to be wrong is failure. And somewhere along the way she got the message that the art of correcting minor details makes you somehow more important or valuable.

Do you sometimes catch yourself playing the role of the Must Be? If so, you simply *must* write about some of the ways you try to live up to that old message that says if you're not right—you're "not enough." *Some of the ways I play the role of the Must Be include* (i.e., the way I tend to interrupt my co-workers' presentations with corrections, the way I correct minor details of my child's story, the way I allow "being right" to cost me in my relationships, etc.) . . . _____

_____

_____

_____

_____

_____

Instead of playing the role of the Must Be, I learned from Dr. Wayne Dyer to "think about being *kind* instead of right." That nugget of wisdom has helped me so much. I know it can help you too. *Write* on. *Ways I can turn my "overconfidence" into kindness, instead of "self-right-ness" include* (i.e., giving credit to my co-workers and not having to contribute in every presentation, celebrating my child's individuality by allowing her to tell stories "her way," learning to weigh the value of being kind over being right, etc.) . . . _____

_____

_____

_____

_____

_____

After "standing in front of the mirror" and looking at the different roles, you may see that you definitely fit into more than one role. Don't worry. That doesn't mean you have some sort of multiple personality disorder. In addition to *my* Perfectionist, Performer, and Must Be roles, I've found myself playing most of the above roles at one time or another.

Just remember, these roles aren't good or bad in moderation.

They are roles that we as women need to understand, because when you're finally able to see the roles you've chosen to play—and their corresponding messages or "scripts"—you can see how you've arrived where you are today. And that knowledge is key to keeping you in the driver's seat so you can move in the direction of your goals and dreams.

The Value of Professional Therapy

With all this focus on our messages from the past, I suspect you may be wondering if I'm about to suggest you need years of professional therapy to really understand what happened to you eons ago. Well, I do believe therapy can help everyone. And if you can afford it and choose to pursue that avenue, great! But if professional therapy is your desire, I recommend that you be relentless in finding an excellent, highly recommended counselor before you begin an extended therapy program.

I have not written this to send you into therapy. In fact, a lot of us can use therapy as a crutch to avoid taking action. We become so fascinated with studying ourselves—trying to find that one "aha" moment in our past that explains who we are—that we forget about driving forward down our road of life.

We can only analyze our parents and our history to a certain extent, and then we must consciously choose to go forward. We don't need years of therapy to come to the conclusion that we've been bombarded by self-doubt. I'm not saying we should try to find someone to blame. Self-doubt just happens. And it happens in every kind of family. No one is immune, no matter what his or her socioeconomic background. Period.

And if that's not enough, we inherit many "shoulds" from childhood too, no matter what type of family we grew up in. The *should* list is endless: what kind of morals we *should* have, what kind of vocation we *should* pursue, what type of personality we *should* have, how we *should* act on our jobs, how we *should* raise our children, how we *should* spend money, how we *should* save it—and so on.

Although so many conditions in our lives have changed, those childhood "shoulds" continue to speak inside us—guiding and controlling the decisions we make, pushing us out of the driver's seat into the passenger side. You can decide for yourself whether or not professional therapy will be a part of your journey toward believing in yourself again.

I simply want to reassure you that—therapy or no therapy—you are capable of staying the course, regardless of the direction or distance you choose.

Overhauling

Your Life

How to Harness
the Renewing Power of
Your True Voice

Depending on how well it's been maintained, your car's engine may power you for 100,000 to 200,000 miles, or even more. Or it may give out within the first 50,000 miles. The same goes for your "inner engine."

In the automotive world, an engine overhaul is the replacement of worn parts in the engine block. In the same sense, your DISCOVERY JOURNAL is designed to help you replace your inner engine's worn-out scripts and negative roles with shiny new attitudes and positive action.

Most of us come to a point in life when it's simply time to overhaul the way we think about ourselves. One of the definitions for the word "overhaul" is: "to renovate, revise, or renew thoroughly." I like the sound of the word *renew*. For me, the thought of being renewed carries with it a sense of hope and positive energy—the kind that can take you far.

Life is brimming with opportunities for renewal.

For one, with every sunrise we're handed a brand-new day. New jobs, new hometowns, new relationships (even a new haircut!) can give us the feeling of being renewed. The births of our son and daughter were definite moments of spiritual renewal in my life. And in my own journey to believing in myself again, the

daily experience of practicing the principles in this very DISCOV-
ERY JOURNAL has made my life a *journey of renewal*.

You, too, are creating your own journey of renewal as you
journal your way through these pages to transform self-doubt into
self-confidence. You're going to face some of your old fears about
change. And as you practice listening to the voice of your true
self you'll learn how to "turn the key" of self-confidence to start
your engine each day. You're also going to focus on your positives, build your self-esteem, and learn anew to love yourself. And
you'll harness the force of habit as you learn some new positive
practices that will help you turn your mind into a great motiva-
tional center to keep you aimed in the right direction.

**Just as muscles are developed—with the right attitude and
the commitment to perform these "overhaul your life" exercises—you *will* see dramatic results.** You will continue on your
way to rediscovering your own hopes and dreams along the road
of renewal. The road to *positively you!*

I Know That Voice from Somewhere

It's time to position your true voice center stage. I want you to
put yourself into the part and really get into this next "vocalizing"
exercise. It will help you warm up for the rest of the journey.

Deep inside you, there is a voice crying out. If you're not
sure you hear it, imagine for the moment that you do. Exactly
what is the voice saying? It is pleading with you to travel beyond
the zone of self-doubt and anxiety. It is begging you to take con-

trol of your steering wheel and choose your own road through life.

It is the voice of your true self.

If you haven't listened to that voice in a very long time, it may sound rather unfamiliar—like a new voice. But, believe me, it has been there all along. It is *positively you*.

Do you hear it?

If not, think back. Visualize that Grand Canyon image, the one where you imagined your true self calling to you from across the vast expanse between the "you" others are allowed to see and the "you" that remains hidden behind your fear of change, your fear of failure, your fear of success.

Now turn down the volume on that voice you've been listening to—the one that's been saying you are destined to stay the way you are for the rest of your life. Instead, imagine this clear strong voice *inside you*—the voice of your true self—telling you that you are destined to succeed.

Say it out loud: I AM DESTINED TO SUCCEED.

Be sure to say it with conviction! Half-heartedly reading it softly to yourself does not count.

I know you may feel silly about doing this at first, but that's only because you're so unaccustomed to hearing such positive messages, much less hearing them in your own voice! You're just going to have to trust me on this. Learning to positively affirm yourself and your journey is going to make a world of difference in the way you feel about you and where you are going in life. Try it again:

I AM DESTINED TO SUCCEED.

Try it with the emphasis on different words and really think about what each word means as you emphasize it:

I AM DESTINED TO SUCCEED.

I AM DESTINED TO SUCCEED.

I AM DESTINED TO SUCCEED.

Now put it in your own handwriting . . . _____

_____

_____

_____

Keep in mind that this is not an exercise to see how well you can speak out loud or how well you can take instruction. You're not just practicing saying the words out loud. You are practicing *believing* what you say. It's the practice of believing in *you*.

Try another one. And remember, you're not just saying it out loud, you're *believing* it out loud.

I AM BETTER THAN I THINK.

Again.

I AM BETTER THAN I THINK.

Now write it out a few times . . . _____

_____

_____

_____

Affirmations work like spark plugs in your car's engine. They're not the be-all and end-all but they can give you just the jolt you need to get going.

Affirmations help you believe in the power you have inside you to change your life. They won't instantly change your life. They won't create some sort of miraculous overnight recovery. But they will give you a "shock" of emotional energy. In fact, you may have shocked yourself just now when you heard yourself say "I am better than I think."

Affirmations startle our senses. They help us begin to break through all that old motor oil and those clogged engine parts that have held us back for so long. A number of women have shared with me how their first practice of self-affirmation was actually quite an emotional experience. It's no wonder.

You may have a similar experience. There's a certain sensation that accompanies the act of using your own voice in such a self-affirming way. It's not unlike the overwhelming sense of delight or surprise that comes with suddenly being called by someone from whom you've not heard in years.

You know how it goes. You answer the phone, you hear the voice, you think to yourself "I *know* that voice from somewhere . . ." and suddenly you realize who's there.

Hellooo. It's Me.

Say hello to your true voice and talk your way through some more *positively you* affirmations. Go ahead. Try this one:

NOTHING CAN STOP ME.

NOTHING CAN STOP ME.

Write this one down now. _____

_____

_____

_____

Doesn't it feel *good* to say those words and put them in writing?!

Think about it. You're here. You've made a commitment to yourself to make this journey to *positively you* a reality. You're spending time with your DISCOVERY JOURNAL every day, or almost every day. You're really working at being more conscious of the way you think, so you can get where you want to go and be who you want to be. This affirmation is a cinch. Say it again:

NOTHING CAN STOP ME. NOTHING CAN STOP ME!

That's good, because if you *choose not* to really live your life, you *lose* an immeasurable treasure. If you don't listen to your true voice—and if you don't heed its call—you miss out on the exhilarating opportunity to display your astonishing uniqueness.

Me? Astonishing? you wonder.

Believe it! No one in the world can do what you can do or think and see the way you think and see things. No one but you can create what you can create. You have far more potential than you even know. But isn't it exciting to know that you're on the road of renewal? You're about to discover the potential that already lies within you. And, if you want, you can create some brand-new potential along the way. Say it out loud and believe it when you say:

I HAVE FAR MORE POTENTIAL THAN I KNOW.

I HAVE FAR MORE POTENTIAL THAN I KNOW.

I HAVE FAR MORE POTENTIAL THAN I KNOW.

Indeed, you do.

Now write it down. _____

_____

_____

_____

As you think up new affirmations for the journey, record them here . . . _____

_____

_____

_____

_____

_____

_____

_____

_____

_____

_____

_____

_____

_____

_____

Just a Note . . . Keep practicing the four affirmations you've just learned. Even on the days when you don't feel so "affirmed," say them anyway. Say them with your best *positively you* fervor. Say them before breakfast. Before a business meeting. Before a mirror! I promise, you will change your thinking and you will have a positive effect on your life. Here they are again:

I am destined to succeed.
I am better than I think.
Nothing can stop me.
I have far more potential than I know.

That's four affirmations, at least three times daily, for as long as negative symptoms persist. Take them along with plenty of patience, self-love, and commitment.

Ready,

Willing,

and Able

Using the
Spark of Confidence
to Transform
Fearing into Steering

Does fear control your life, especially when it comes to growth or change? Does the idea of facing your fears make you want to skip this part?

Quick! Grab onto those affirmations prescribed in the preceding pages. Trust your true voice to fuel your ability to face your fears. And journal your way through the following "vocalizing" exercises. As you break through the barrier of your fears, you will build your confidence to an all-time high. You are about to become more resolved than ever in your commitment to the *positively you* journey.

Brake-Your-Fear, Accelerate-Your-Confidence Exercises

1. Let's say your husband or a friend asks you what you want to do tonight. You reply, "Oh, 'it doesn't matter. Whatever *you* want to do." So the other person says, "Fine. I want to go see that new action adventure movie—the one with all the chase scenes, macho men, and mindless women . . ." You are now stuck going to a movie you don't want to see, and you feel resentful about it.

Just a Note . . . What is courage? Think of it as nothing more than recognizing you are fearful about something—and then doing it anyway.

If you really want something, do you have trouble asking for it? If so, write down some examples of similar scenarios. I have a hard time asking for what I really want (i.e., when I'm out to dinner and the waiter brings the wrong food, when my husband starts watching TV and I'd rather we could talk about what's going on in our lives, when I apply for a new job or a new position at work, etc.) . . . _____

_____

_____

_____

_____

_____

_____

_____

Now, explore what it might be like to actually ask for what you want—and get it! Breaking from your fear to speak up and say what you want in life could cast your relationships—personal and professional—in a whole new light. *If I were to ask for*

what I really want, I could get (i.e., better service in res-
taurants, more attention and better communication from my husband, a raise in pay or the career of my dreams, etc.) . . . _____

_____

_____

_____

_____

_____

_____

_____

_____

_____

Put your affirmations to good use. Listen to your true voice.
And make sure others listen too. As you build your confidence
and learn to believe in *you*, others will sit up and take notice.

**2. Do you talk yourself out of buying a fine antique table
because you fear something might happen to it in your home?**
Maybe you think you're "not worthy" or that you don't deserve
to own nice things. *What do you think this fear is really about?* *I'm
reluctant to purchase anything "too nice" because* (i.e., no
one else in my family spends money on "niceties," I don't really
have the confidence that I deserve it, I'm afraid if something ever
happens to it I will have wasted my money, etc.) . . . _____

_____

_____

_____

_____

_____

_____

_____

_____

F.Y.I.: This is not an exercise to determine how materialistic you can be. And I'm certainly not encouraging you to go into debt! But it *is* telling if you fear you aren't "up to" the finer things in life.

By "finer" I mean that quality by which *you* determine an object's value. As they say in the antique business, "One woman's trash is another's treasure," or something like that. One friend may long to surround herself with classic Italian furnishings, where you may be more into the "shabby chic" craze and saving up to splurge on rare flea market finds.

From the most humble of homes to the most extravagant, what matters is that you place the *highest* value on always "speaking" in your true voice—from the things you say, to the clothes you wear, to the home you create. *When I do treat myself with a personal "treasure" for my home* (i.e., I create a more soulful living space where I can recharge my battery, my guests leave my home feeling like they know me a little better, etc.) . . .

_____

_____

_____
_____
_____
_____
_____
_____
_____
_____
_____
_____

Steering instead of fearing, you can develop all the inner confidence you need to feather your nest and create the home of your dreams.

3. Do you ever talk yourself out of a relationship because you think the person is out of your league (too attractive, too successful, too rich)? Write about that fear. *When I'm afraid to get to know someone, it's usually because* (i.e., I'm so self-critical I think I'll never measure up, I've never had a meaningful relationship that lasted, I just don't have enough confidence in myself, etc.) . . . _____

_____
_____
_____
_____
_____
_____

> *Just a Note . . .* Continuing to "open up" in your journal is great practice
> for opening your life to new and meaningful relationships and experiences. I
> know you will find, as I have, that the *practice* of keeping your thoughts and
> feelings in a journal—truly is one of the most self-affirming and profoundly
> healing actions you will take on your life's journey.
>
>

By now, you've probably noticed a message that continues to surface in these "brake-your-fear" exercises. It's the same underlying negative message found in the roles you wrote about earlier in your DISCOVERY JOURNAL. Remember? The message was that you are "not enough." But that message is false.

Keep on voicing those affirmations and never stop reminding yourself that you are on a "change your thinking" journey. Now write. *Ways I can open up my life to more meaningful relationships include* (i.e., practicing the art of self-affirmation, acknowledging my habit of self-limiting behavior and then reaching out anyway—one small risk at a time, etc.) . . . _____

_____

_____

_____

_____

_____

_____

_____

_____

4. Do you talk yourself out of trying a new activity—like skiing, tennis, tai chi, windsurfing, golf, horseback riding—simply because you don't want to look incompetent in front of other people? *If so, what's that fear all about?* *I avoid the happiness that can come from learning a new activity because* (i.e., I think I need the approval of others to be happy, I'm afraid of failure, I'm afraid of change, etc.) . . . _____

_____

_____

_____

_____

_____

_____

_____

Okay, now picture yourself trying the new activity of your choice. Can you see yourself in action? What's the worst that can happen? *If I try this new activity, the worst thing that can happen might be* (i.e., I feel uncoordinated at first or I lose my balance, I might be a slow learner, I may have to lose more than my share of games before I win one, etc.) . . . _____

_____

_____

_____

_____

_____

_____

Still, with the worst possible scenario in mind, wouldn't you be willing to risk those things in exchange for the incredibly life-affirming energy and confidence that comes with the simple act of trying something new?! I thought so. Write about that. *By saying "yes" to trying this new activity, I am saying "yes!"* (i.e., *to myself* by having confidence in my potential, *to my children* by showing them that they can overcome their fears too, *to life* by not settling for less than what I can be, etc.) . . .

_____

_____

_____

_____

_____

_____

Just a Note . . . I understand that your daily schedule already may be so full you just can't imagine adding a "new activity" to the mix. All I want to say about that is this: the point is to not get in a *changeless* rut. If you're already in a rut—say you've been walking the same route in your neighborhood for years—do your self-confidence a world of good and make a change. Walk a new path. Call up a friend and go hit some tennis balls. Heck, why not give rollerblading a try, with your niece, child, or grandchild as coach! *Finding new ways to activate your confidence will help you break old fears.*

_____

_____

_____

_____

_____

Good! Now don't wait for that new "activity opportunity" to come knocking at your door. Actively go and seek it out. Chanting your affirmations all the way: "I am destined to succeed; I am better than I think; Nothing can stop me; and I have far more potential than I know."

5. Do you tell yourself that you can't lose weight because you don't have the willpower? Or because your metabolism doesn't work the way it did when you were younger? *What are you really afraid of? I tell myself I can't lose weight because* (i.e., I'm afraid of the lifestyle changes I'll have to make to be more fit, I'm afraid I'll fail, I'm afraid I'll succeed, etc.) . . . _____

_____

_____

_____

_____

_____

_____

_____

Keep telling yourself you "can't" do something, and sure enough, you'll talk yourself out of success. Next time you get stuck in that nagging "can't do" voice, instead of your encouraging "can-do" voice, practice your affirmations. A good one to focus on is the one that says, "I am destined to succeed."

Just think what you stand to gain by losing the unhealthy weight you've been talking yourself into all these years. *When I lose my extra weight, I'll gain so much in the way of* (i.e., my personal sense of accomplishment, my health and overall sense of well-being, getting in practice for making other positive changes in my life, etc.) . . . _____

_____

_____

_____

_____

_____

_____

_____

_____

With every positively affirming word you speak, you will generate all the energy, willingness, and *emotional metabolism* you need to attain and maintain the weight that is healthy for you. You are "destined to succeed."

6. Do you ever say to yourself that you're too old to try something new? Okay, you're far enough into these exercises by now that you know this is a fear-based conclusion you've reached—based totally on your imagination. And prematurely at that, since you gave up before you even tried the new thing. Am I right? If I am, it's only because I've done this to myself more than a time or two. Write about whatever that "new thing" is you've secretly longed to try but talked yourself out of. Describe it in detail. The *"something new" I've been telling myself I'm too old to try is* (i.e., getting a computer and learning how to use it, going back to school for a degree in psychology, starting a new business out of my home, dating again, etc.) . . . _____

_____

_____

_____

_____

_____

_____

_____

_____

Now write about some ways you can "test the waters." *Some specific steps I can take in the direction of trying something new include* (i.e., scheduling some time to observe a computer-literate friend at work, visiting the campus of my local college or university and meeting with a professor, tapping into a "work-at-home" network of people, telling the people who know me best that I'm interested in meeting some new gentlemen friends, etc.) . . . _____

_____

_____

_____

_____

_____

_____

_____

_____

Still not sure? Look. Just think for a moment how you regard *others* who try new things. You admire them, don't you? They inspire you, right? Even when they stumble or fail, their spirit of adventure and their willingness to learn and grow uplifts you. *You can do this.* Remember, you "have far more potential than you know."

7. Do you believe you don't have enough *time* to master some-thing new, even though medical studies now say a fifty-year-old female without cancer or heart disease probably will live to the age of ninety-two? None of us really know how much time we have to live our lives. But go ahead and explore this for minute. *What are your fears? I'm afraid if I try to master something new I'll run out of time because* (i.e., I struggle with health problems, I'm a slow learner, I procrastinate, etc.) . . .

_____

_____

_____

_____

_____

_____

_____

_____

_____

The way I see it, being afraid you'll run out of time is pretty much a waste of time. Instead, think about just how long you actually may live. Do you want to spend those years staying on the road you're traveling? Can you see how "change" could im-prove the quality of the years you have before you?

Write about the prospect of your life*time* spent in a state of fulfillment instead of fearfulness. *When I stop worrying about the days to come and start living the day at hand, I* *can focus on* (i.e., making the most of each day, pursuing my dreams instead of putting them off, taking a specific step toward trying something new, etc.) . . . _____

_____

_____

_____

_____

_____

_____

_____

It really does make a difference when you choose to see the glass as half full instead of half empty. Just remember the affirmation "Nothing can stop me." Then take off your watch and go live your life!

8. Do you have difficulty enjoying a pleasurable moment because you constantly think about what you *should* be doing instead? You might want to refer back to where you explored the power of "roles" and how those childhood "shoulds" continue to speak inside you. *What do you think you're really afraid of?* Start writing and see what you can discover about yourself—and your "shoulds." *Maybe the reason I can't let myself enjoy a moment's peace is because* (i.e., I'm afraid things will get out of control if I don't constantly work, I was often reprimanded for not working hard enough as a child so now I overdo it, I'm afraid if I stop and smell the roses something bad will happen, etc.) . . . _____

_____

_____

_____

_____

_____

_____

_____

_____

Now switch gears and practice steering instead of fearing. Describe some of your potentially pleasurable moments. What do they look like? *For me, a pleasurable moment could be something as simple as* (i.e., taking a luxurious hot bath instead of a fast on-the-go shower, eating my lunch in a nearby park instead of in the company break room, waking up thirty minutes before the rest of my family to enjoy some quiet time for myself, etc.) . . . _____

_____

_____

_____

_____

_____

_____

_____

_____

_____

_____

As you review the moments you just described, do any of them require that much of your time or energy? Who or what will *really* suffer if you don't attend to all your shoulds before you allow yourself a pleasurable moment? It's you and the ones you love who suffer most when you don't mindfully create moments of renewal throughout the days and weeks of your busy life. But, hey! You're creating such a moment right now as you journal along. It's good practice for the journey.

What Was *That*? It Felt Like a Tremor!

No sweat. You're heading toward solid ground. As you worked through those last exercises, you were little by little tapping the brakes—putting a stop to those pesky fears that have been building up a wall between you and your dreams.

It's smart to be aware, though, that as you begin to grow beyond your internal negative messages and fears, you actually unsettle the foundation upon which you have built your self-image. And that can be, well—unsettling!

Subconsciously, you may feel a bit edgy, even downright uncomfortable. Why? Because those familiar negative voices are giving way to a new voice. Your true voice.

I know you're probably wondering, "Wait a minute, Jinger. I thought all these exercises for getting in touch with my true inner voice were going to make me feel better, not worse!"

Believe me, life does get so much better when you're "in voice." But what's ironic is that whenever we try to start our engines—when we begin to transform ourselves and bring success into our lives—it's not at all unusual to feel greater levels of anxiety for a while.

The reason? Frankly, for many of us, personal transformation and success are unfamiliar experiences—that means, at the very first sign of our moving toward change, we feel like stopping right then and there. After all, we try to avoid anxiety, right? So instead of embracing the sound of our true voice and the better choices that voice can inspire us to make, we hold back and stay within the parameters of our safety zones.

We fear instead of steer. We stop growing and changing. And although doing nothing results in the greatest failure of all, it apparently is easier for many of us to accept passive rather than active failure.

What's that? You say you've been there and done that and now you're willing to make a true commitment to change? Great. Willingness absolutely is the key to starting your engine. If you really are willing—you really will.

By this point of your journey you know all too well that you can't wait for the spirit to move you or until you feel "just right." And how many people do you know who, because of their circumstances, think they have no personal power or control to change the direction of their own lives?

Are you one of those people? If you are, excuse me, but you're wrong about you. Your happiness and success in life do not depend on your circumstances but on how you respond to your circumstances. And how you respond has everything in the world to do with how you choose to think about yourself and your life.

If you simply are willing to get going, you can work on your inner-life changes in the same way you work on a muscle. The more you work on it, the more its performance improves. And just as important to keep in mind, the more you leave it alone, the more out of shape it gets. What better "muscle" set to work on for overcoming fears than those "thinking muscles" that have to do with your confidence!

So stay warmed up and ready to work out. You're going to be exercising those muscles quite a bit from now on.

Voicing Your Confidence

Do you recognize how well practiced you are at tuning into the voices of everyone but you? Think about it. You're constantly tuned into others' voices at your job, in your home, and through the media.

Staying attuned to your own voice is going to take some

> *Just a Note . . .* I confess—I talk to myself. I know people say that's a sign of craziness, but I beg to differ. When I hear my thoughts *in my voice* instead of just in my head, the sound of my voice actually "revs up" my consciousness. Try it sometime. Read sections of your DISCOVERY JOURNAL out loud. Or tell yourself your plans for the day. As empowering as it is to put your thoughts in writing, it's equally energizing to hear them out loud. Get to know *you* and the startling clarity that comes from using your voice.
>
>

practice too. Of course, that's what keeping a journal is all about. But in previous exercises, your DISCOVERY JOURNAL has provided most of the "what if" scenarios and you have responded in your own voice. Now it's your turn to initiate things.

The following space is a place for you to name three very real fears—big or little—and then claim your true voice as you write about some specific ways you can move toward each fear, embrace it, and turn it into an opportunity for positive change.

Here's a fictitious example to help you get started:

NAMING MY FEAR: *I have a real fear of job interviews. I always freeze up once I get there. I feel self-conscious and then I forget to ask important questions.*

VOICING MY CONFIDENCE: *Instead of avoiding interviews, I will pursue them! I will prepare by doing things like dress rehearsals, practicing confident posture, listing my questions* *ahead of time and practicing my self-affirmation statements to boost my confidence.*

NAMING MY FEAR: _____

_____

_____

_____

_____

_____

VOICING MY CONFIDENCE: _____

_____

_____

_____

_____

_____

_____

_____

_____

NAMING MY FEAR: _____

_____

_____

_____

_____

VOICING MY CONFIDENCE: _____

_____

_____

_____

_____

_____

_____

_____

_____

_____

NAMING MY FEAR: _____

_____

_____

_____

_____

VOICING MY CONFIDENCE: _____

_____

_____

_____

_____

_____

_____

_____

_____

_____

Risky Business

Keep practicing and you'll grow accustomed to naming your fears and voicing your confidence. Then, use this next journal space to record some of the risks you take—big and little ones—as you journey away from fear and toward *positively you*.

It's important to make notes about your progress. For one, it helps you pay attention, which helps when you're working on changing your thinking. And it's encouraging to occasionally go back and read sections from your DISCOVERY JOURNAL. It'll make you smile to yourself about the amazing journey of life. What's more, by making time to write about these things, you are giving yourself the honor and respect that you deserve.

RISK SPECIFICS—JUST FOR THE RECORD: *Here are some of the big and little risks I'm taking as I name my fears and voice my confidence to move in a new direction . . .*

_____

_____

_____

_____

_____

Just a Note... There's nothing like a little risk taking to build your confidence. I remember learning to ski and being so afraid of falling. But if you want to be a good skier, you have to lean past what's called the "fall line." Only when I chose to go with gravity and risk skiing in a way that made me feel like I was going to fall did I realize I wasn't going to fall at all. Instead, I flew down the hill without resistance. That's steering instead of fearing. It's worth the risk.

The Road to Wholeness
Is Paved with Willingness

Isn't it incredible how energized you become when you stare your fears in the face, exercise your voice of confidence, and willingly take a risk? What a relief to know you can transform that all-too-familiar pool of stagnant fear and negativity into a lively wellspring of energy and change for the better.

When it comes to starting your engine and facing your old fears about change, there is no magic formula for change except the willingness to change. That means the willingness to risk and do something about your fears. You are taking that risk *right now!* And that proves your ability to face fears and make changes—not just on paper, but in real life. Believe that about yourself, because it is true. By taking a risk in one area, this DIS-COVERY JOURNAL for example, you are becoming more confident about taking risks in other ways.

Indeed, regardless of where we are in life, we can make significant changes by initially taking very small risks and then moving to larger ones.

Never be afraid of fear. As you start changing, don't run from your fear. Move toward it instead. Embrace it even.

The alternative?

The more you avoid or resist the things you fear, the more you will stay the same. Besides, this is not the "same-old-you" DISCOVERY JOURNAL. As I've reminded you before, it's the *positively you* one.

Hey! Here are a few new affirmations to add to your list. Try them on for size:

I AM WILLING TO CONFRONT MY FEAR.

I AM ABLE TO VOICE MY CONFIDENCE.

I AM READY, WILLING, AND ABLE TO STAY THE COURSE.

Well, *of course*, you are.

Just a Note . . . It's important that you begin to prepare your mind for the road beyond the journal writing you're doing here. I encourage you to acknowledge to yourself now that you deserve to continue the practice of keeping a journal long after you've filled the pages of this one. If you weren't already in the habit of journalizing, my hope is that your *Positively You!* DISCOVERY JOURNAL will serve as one great big warm-up exercise. A lifelong practice of staying in touch with your true voice—through the simple act of writing in a journal—will give you a limitless life-changing supply of fuel for the journey.

Staying

the Course

How to Transform
Positively You Thinking
into Meaningful Action

I know you're ready to take this rediscovered belief in yourself and let it carry you where you want to go in life. That's why *now* is the time to get your "wheels" in balance, so you can be on your way and stay the course.

When I was a child, my father taught me what turned out to be one of my most valuable life lessons: **If the four wheels of your car aren't balanced, you're in for a bumpy ride.** It's simple, but so true. Without balanced wheels, your car pulls to one side or the other. Next thing you know, you find yourself losing control of what and how you want your life to be.

All four wheels need focus. The wheels represent the four main areas of life in which we all strive for balance—Work, Home, People, and Self. You'll recall writing along these lines on pages 23–25.

The following exercise will help you use your own calendar or day planner to assess the ways you currently spend time in these areas. With that clear picture, you'll be ready to map out some doable goals to help you attain and maintain the kind of "four-wheel balance" you need to keep your day-to-day life moving in the direction of your dreams.

Balance Assessment 101

Ready to create an at-a-glance "picture" of your life's balances and imbalances? This is an easy exercise that will really open your eyes. Using your own calendar or day planner, simply jot down the details of what you do in an average week. Make note of as many specific actions as you can reasonably make time for in the course of a busy day. That means you're going to record little things like the ten minutes you spend reading the morning paper while having breakfast. Or the fifteen minutes you spend talking with your child while you drive him or her to school. The lunch meeting you have with a friend. The chunks of time you devote to work. The breaks you take for daydreaming.

The more specific you can get, the clearer your "picture" will be. At the end of the seven days, use four different-colored highlighter pens to color-code your calender pages. Don't feel as though you need to spend too much time with this color-coding process. It's simply a tool I've found helpful in keeping my own balance in check.

The idea is for each color to represent a different wheel. For example, I use green to highlight the activities that relate to my Work Wheel, because I associate the color green with money and growth. I highlight activities that relate to my Self Wheel with yellow. That color makes me think of sunshine and times that replenish my spirit. For the times I spend with my daughter, Brittany, I use the color pink to designate my Home Wheel. And so on. Choose colors that are meaningful to you.

Keeping track of how you spend the minutes of your days may be a challenging task, but it pays big dividends. Those calendar pages will clearly show your true colors where life's imbalances are concerned. And with that picture in hand, you'll see what actions you need to take to achieve a more balanced palette of possibilities! Have a good week.

Balance Analysis

No doubt, you made some new discoveries about your life as you color-coded your days. Do you see a definite overabundance of the Work Wheel color in your life? Or do you have a nice rainbow of colors on most days? With the past seven days fresh on your mind and your calendar at your side, now would be a good time to write down some observations about the insights you've gained from this coloring exercise.

As you put your analysis into words, you'll get an even clearer vision of how you can use your seven-day calendar assessment as a powerful balancing tool. *As I look at the way I've "colored" my life during the past week, the following things really stand out* (i.e., I spend hours focusing for too long in one area when I could have used that time to be more constructive in another area, sometimes I'm not really "present" with friends or with my children because I'm always thinking about other things I need to be doing, I don't set clear boundaries for each significant wheel in my life, etc.) . . . _____

_____

_____

_____

_____

_____

Now take your balance analysis a step further. Referring back to your calendar colors, write down your observations specific to each of the four areas.

I notice that when it comes to my Self Wheel (i.e., I seem to put this area last) . . . _____

_____

_____

_____

_____

When it comes to making time for the relationships in my People Wheel (i.e., I struggle with not being able to relax and just be myself) . . . _____

_____

_____

_____

_____

According to my balance assessment of the past week, the time I put in toward my Work Wheel tells me (i.e., I allow a few difficult work relationships to control my attitude) . . .

_____

_____

_____

_____

_____

_____

And as I review the time I devote to my Home Wheel, I can see that (i.e., I have placed home chores above playing with my children) . . . _____

_____

_____

_____

_____

The Art of Scheduling Balance

What's clear to a lot of people who go through a color-coding exercise is that a large reason for unbalanced lives is a lack of planning.

I know from experience that the best way for me to stay in balance is to *schedule it.* That's not to say I spend perfectly equal amounts of time in every important area of my life. Still, I do schedule balance into my days. I set aside special times in the morning to work out (part of my Self Wheel), and certain afternoons and evenings to spend time *only* with my family (Home Wheel). I schedule my time at the office, where I ask my assistant to monitor any personal calls (Work Wheel), as well as time with our closest friends (People Wheel). It's my way of checking on the alignment of my "car" to keep the wheels balanced.

At the start of each week, I write down everything I want to do that week for the four different areas of my life. Then, on my calendar, I try to find places to focus purely on those wheels. I choose a couple of hours on a certain afternoon each week, for example, to be with my daughter. I don't worry about it cutting into my work time. I create another place on my calendar to get in those two extra hours of work.

Believe me, if I can do this, you can do this. And I encourage you to do just that toward the end of this chapter with another seven-day balance assessment. Only the next time you can try practicing the art of scheduling balance *before* you launch into your week! It'll be exciting to see the transformation. But first . . .

The Road to Becoming *Positively You* Is Paved with Goals

When it comes to setting goals to help you believe in yourself again and move in the direction of your dreams—well, you've practically written a book about that very thing! Now that you've just about filled up your DISCOVERY JOURNAL, I want to help you see how to turn what you've written into real goals that can help lead you toward a balanced life.

The exercise of goal setting is more satisfying—and certainly more balanced—when you get really specific about the goals for each of your four areas of life. It's especially important to develop

> *Just a Note . . .* Keep in mind, your four wheels of life encompass a range of goal possibilities. The Work Wheel includes goals that have to do with your job, volunteer work or if you're a stay-at-home mom—that's certainly a full-time job! The Home Wheel involves goals that have to do with your relationship with your family, as well as goals related to homemaking and creating your own special sanctuary for living. The People Wheel goals concern your relationships with friends and co-workers. And the Self Wheel is a place to attach goals that relate to your physical, emotional, and spiritual well-being.
>
>

smaller, short-term goals that help you stay the course toward fulfilling each long-term goal.

Setting specific goals for your four "wheels" of life is a surefire way to transform *"positively you* thinking" into meaningful *action.* Ready to start? You're about to begin the exercise of connecting goals to your wheels. You'll do that by referencing your own writing from the thoughts and feelings you've recorded on earlier pages.

Mining for Goals

This exercise works like a treasure map of sorts. The chapter and page number references point the way. All you have to do is thumb back through the pages, rediscover the "goal nuggets" you wrote in your journal along the way, then jot them down in the spaces provided in this section. When you finish mining for goals, you'll "attach" specific goals to each of your four wheels on the Life Goals "Balance" Sheet near the end of this chapter. Your completed balance sheet will provide you with the perfect at-a-glance guide to help you plan your days as you practice scheduling balance and staying the course.

Enjoy *rediscovering* the wealth of goals you've already written in your DISCOVERY JOURNAL!

Your "Mining for Goals" Treasure Map

This exercise is a breeze. These next few pages give you a step-by-step, page-by-page guide to all the great goals you've *already written*. Take this opportunity to simply flip back and "capture" them in the spaces provided. When you're done, you will have "stored" all your goals here in this simple location where they'll be easy to refer back to for years to come.

Go to the "Preparing for the Journey" chapter, page 20.

Refer to #3, Your Dreams. It's here in this Top 10 Bring-Alongs exercise that you began to reconnect with your dreams and to redirect your path. The dreams you wrote about were more than likely long–term goals. If those dreams still resonate for you, record them here now as they relate to one of the four wheels. Feel free to write down *new* long-term goals as well. (*Note: Just as the condition of one wheel on a car effects all the other* *wheels, so can one goal apply to more than one wheel. Still, it's important to attach each goal to the primary wheel it influences.)*

WORK WHEEL LONG-TERM GOALS: _____

_____

_____

_____

_____

_____

_____

_____

_____

HOME WHEEL LONG-TERM GOALS: _____

_____

_____

_____

_____

_____

_____

_____

_____

PEOPLE WHEEL LONG-TERM GOALS: _____

_____

_____

_____

_____

_____

_____

_____

_____

_____

SELF WHEEL LONG-TERM GOALS: _____

_____

_____

_____

_____

_____

_____

_____

_____

Refer to #6, Balance, page 23. Here's the place I referred to earlier where you first began to write about specific actions you could take to bring balance to each of your four wheels. I think you'll find it interesting to go back and read what you wrote then. Keep the ones you still feel strongly about and translate them into short-term goals for each wheel. I've given you a little more space for these. That's because for every long-term goal listed above, you'll more than likely come up with numerous short-term goals to keep you on course.

WORK WHEEL SHORT-TERM GOALS: _____

_____

_____

_____

_____

_____

_____

_____

_____

_____

_____

HOME WHEEL SHORT-TERM GOALS: _____

_____

_____

_____

_____

_____

_____

_____

_____

_____

_____

_____

PEOPLE WHEEL SHORT-TERM GOALS: _____

_____

_____

_____

_____

_____

_____

_____

_____

_____

_____

_____

SELF WHEEL SHORT-TERM GOALS: _____

_____

_____

_____

_____

_____

_____

Great! Now that you've established your basic long-term and short-term goals, you can take it a step further if you like. Following are additional "goal mines" you've written along the way. Glance back over the referenced passages and you'll discover more goals, which you easily can add to those you recorded in the lists above.

Go to the "Learning to Believe in Yourself Again" chapter, page 40.

Refer to the Tune-up Exercises. You'll recall this is where you began to consider what you want your life to be like one year from now and five years from now—more long-term goals. What's more, you wrote down specific ways to reach those goals—more short-term goals. Again, it's been a while and you've "traveled" some distance since the journalizing you did earlier in the book. If some of your goals have evolved into new ones, that's okay! Take what you find there and translate them into goals for today.

Go to the "Finding the Way, Going the Distance" chapter, page 49.

Refer to the Put Yourself on the Map Exercises. Take some cues about other goals to consider here in the Who Am I? and Where Am I Going? exercises. Don't be surprised if your answers to these questions have changed along the way. Celebrate the *renewed you* and renew your goals!

Refer to the More "Finding Yourself" Exercises, page 52. Jump down to where you journaled: "I have often dreamed of . . ." After all, dreams are what long-term goals are made of!

Then move on to page 55. Refer to where you journaled "I'm going to make some new choices . . ." There you'll find some short-term goals just waiting to be connected to one of your wheels of life.

Refer to A Few Practice Steering Exercises, page 58. Look— more goals!

Go to the "Check Under the Hood" chapter, page 66.

Refer to the "Remember the Time . . . ?" section. There (on page 64), you'll find the entry "I will begin to re-create 'at-my-best' moments when . . ." Once again, I think you'll find some short-term goals just waiting to happen.

Go to the "In the Driver's Seat" chapter, page 84.

Refer to the "Role Call" section. You remember the Caged Spirit, the Pretty Woman, and the Procrastinator, don't you?! In the second part of each role described, you wrote specific ways to play up the strengths inherent to that role. As you reread each one, you'll pick up some more goals to connect to your wheels. And while you're there, harness the power of those positive traits to achieve your goals!

Go to the "Overhauling Your Life" chapter, page 116.

Refer to the four affirmations reviewed in the Note at the end of the chapter. You won't find any goals here. But I just had to point you back to this place and remind you to tap your own inner wellspring of motivation! I promise, if you'll use these affirmations, plus any new ones you've written along the way, you will have an endless supply of confidence and focus as you strive to accomplish your goals and bring balance to your days.

Go to the "Ready, Willing, and Able" chapter, page 119.

Refer to the Brake-Your-Fear, Accelerate-Your-Confidence Exercises. Direct your attention to the solution-oriented second half of each exercise. As you review, you'll find many of the thoughts you recorded there can easily be transformed into more short-term goals to connect to your wheels.

Refer to the Voicing Your Confidence exercises, page 136. You'll discover more "goal nuggets" in the "Voicing My Con-

Just a Note . . . Setting goals *is* risky business, by the way, because you're getting very specific with yourself about your desires. Next thing you know, people are telling you, "Don't take risks," and "You'll be better off if you just play it safe," or "You might fail if you try." When that happens, you know what to do. Turn down the volume on those negative messages, voice your positive affirmations, and *take some action, no matter how small it is.* For years at work, I've seen what this attitude can accomplish. Thousands of women in our company have come to believe in the simple practice of setting short-term and long-term goals in life. By accomplishing a goal, your feelings about yourself will change. You will know what it's like to believe in yourself again.

fidence" writing you did following each "Naming My Fear" journal space.

And finally, refer to the Risky Business exercise on page 140. It's here you began to record some of the risks you're taking as you move away from fear and toward *positively you.* The risks you wrote about can easily join your list of ongoing short-term goals.

Putting Your Life Goals in Balance

Now that you've mined the goals from your journal writing, I think you'll find it especially rewarding to place your goals on the following Life Goals "Balance" Sheet. Simply refer to the long-term and short-term goals you listed on pages 155–159 and position them on the appropriate lines adjacent to each wheel. When you've completed filling in the sheet, you will have created a dynamic picture of the balance and direction you are striving toward on your journey to becoming *positively you.* Have fun creating this powerful visual tool!

LIFE GOALS "BALANCE" SHEET

Long-Term Goals

_____

_____

_____

_____

Short-Term Goals

_____

_____

_____

_____

Long-Term Goals

_____

_____

_____

_____

Short-Term Goals

_____

_____

_____

_____

Long-Term Goals

_____

_____

_____

_____

Short-Term Goals

_____

_____

_____

_____

Long-Term Goals

_____

_____

_____

_____

Short-Term Goals

_____

_____

_____

_____

WORK **HOME**

Positively YOU!

PEOPLE **SELF**

Color Your Life with Balance

This final exercise is the perfect way to bring your DISCOVERY JOURNAL to a close and send you on your way to new horizons. It's the other seven-day balance assessment I promised you. Only this time we're going to call it a seven-day balance "plan," because you're going to practice the art of *scheduling* balance—remember?!

This exercise isn't about looking back. It's about looking ahead and, with boldness, making a commitment to yourself to go where you want to go.

Using the preceding balance sheet as the *positively you* "vision" for changing your life, grab your calendar and your highlighter pens and, this time, color your life with balance. *Plan* the balance and short-term goals into your schedule *before* you launch into the next seven days.

Plan your week, *live* the plan, and while you're at it, *please* remember to allow for some spontaneity!

I wish I could be there to celebrate with you at the end of the seven days—to cheer you onward and upward. As I draw this chapter to a close, and you continue on the path to *positively you*, I am filled with the kind of anticipation one has when waiting for a friend to open a gift.

I *know*—even if you don't quite sense it yet—any day now you're going to smile to yourself and realize that somewhere along the way you truly have begun to believe in yourself again.

How do I know that? Just look at you there with your planner and your pens.

You are transforming your *positively you* **thinking into meaningful action!** And here's an important "driving" tip for the road ahead: *Be prepared for flat tires.* Experienced drivers know flat tires are a normal part of the journey. No car, regardless of how good it is, can go forever without one of its tires losing air. A flat tire doesn't mean your car is broken. You simply fix the tire and move on. So consider a mistake you make in life as nothing more than a flat tire. I try to follow what I call the "80–20" rule. It helps put my "flat tires" in perspective.

Here's the idea. After you color-code your calendar and look back on it, celebrate the days where you have accomplished your balance or goals 80 percent of the time. It's reassuring and motivating to look back over a week, month, or even a year and enjoy the satisfaction of seeing how—a good 80 percent of the time—you've lived and worked toward your goals in a balanced way. If you've met 80 percent of your Self Wheel goals for working out, that's excellent. If you've accomplished 80 percent of your Work Wheel or People Wheel goals, that's incredible!

Sometimes you'll fall short. But you know what? That's okay! It's just a flat tire. Even if the colors on your calendar reveal that you aren't making the 80 percent, you *are* making progress. What you've already written in this DISCOVERY JOURNAL is so wonderful. You are moving forward. Celebrate that.

Remember, you're human and this is all about awareness— *not* perfection.

The New *Positively You*

Congratulations! You've completed your DISCOVERY JOURNAL *and* experienced your first week of scheduling goals and balance into your days.

Celebrate how far you've come. You're learning to believe in yourself again. You're in the driver's seat. And you're staying the course.

You are making up your mind and moving in the direction of your dreams. And that is what being *positively you* is all about.

Use this next journal space to write any final observations, thoughts, or meditations about the journey that has brought you to this point in time. Perhaps you'd like to bring this to a close by writing some new affirmations to inspire you onward. Or maybe you'd like to write a letter to the new *positively you*.

Whatever is in your heart, write it here. Then, when you're down the road a bit, come back and reread some of the passages you've written. This DISCOVERY JOURNAL will always be a source of strength—a personal testimony of your belief in yourself. A place where you started making your dreams come true . . . _____

_____

_____

_____

_____

_____

_____

_____

_____

_____

_____

_____

_____

_____

_____

_____

_____

_____

_____

_____

_____

_____

_____

_____

_____

_____

_____

_____

_____

_____

_____ *positively! to be continued . . .*

Epilogue

The Joy
of the
Journey

In bringing this to a close, I want to say, God bless you. Not just for the great distance you have journeyed thus far, but for the discoveries you've yet to make and the positive life changes you've mapped out for yourself.

The well-lived life is not a destination but a journey.

And the joy of the journey is as much about the adventure as it is about the arriving. Celebrate the slow, steady change. The destination will take care of itself.

Your dedication will pay off.

Already, you've learned so many valuable lessons and new skills to help you stay the course to *positively you*. Simply learning and living these lessons is what happens when you commit to a course of action.

I can just picture you now. You've grabbed hold of the wheel. And you're burning rubber on the way from self-doubt to self-confidence. You are a woman on a mission. You've begun the work. You've answered the tough questions and the easy ones, which will provide you with an endless supply of fuel for the journey.

The payoff?

You are making life-changing discoveries.

You are transforming your thoughts and dreams into meaningful action.

Godspeed, sister traveler. I look forward to seeing you along the way as we each continue to experience the joy of the journey.

J. L. H.

About Jinger L. Heath

Committed to women's total health and well-being, Jinger Heath is the Co-Founder and Chairman of BeautiControl® Cosmetics, a global direct sales company with more than 60,000 Image Consultants who specialize in personalized head-to-toe image solutions. As chairman, speaker, author, and philanthropist, Ms. Heath has inspired and empowered thousands of women to make positive choices and be all they can be.

In 1993, Ms. Heath founded the national WHO® Foundation out of her philosophy, Women Helping Others. The foundation has awarded more than a million dollars to women's and children's charities. In addition to *Positively You!* and *The Positively You! Discovery Journal*, Ms. Heath is the author of two critical health guides for women, distributed by the WHO Foundation. As a result of her work on behalf of women everywhere, Ms. Heath was recently nominated as an "Influential Woman of the 21st Century" in Lifetime network's online presentation, "Women of the Century." She has appeared on *Oprah*, *The View with Barbara Walters*, *The Montel Williams Show*, and other numerous programs.

Ms. Heath has been married to her soul mate and best friend, BeautiControl Co-Founder and CEO Richard Heath, for twenty-six years. They live in Dallas, Texas, and have four children.